PRAISE FOR **COURAGE OVER FEAR**

"HR leaders sit in the tension between culture and performance, strategy and humanity. *Courage Over Fear* is a rallying cry for those of us helping leaders navigate their most pivotal moments—not with scripts, but with guts, grace, and values in action. This book turns pressure into a proving ground for courageous leadership. It belongs in every HR leader's toolkit."

—Laura Grose, HRBP, VP, Entertainment Company

"Kristen and Mike leverage their experience leading DEI and talent development at Tesla to show us how courageous leaders can take ownership of their roles and create progress in a fear-driven environment. Today, more than ever, we need that kind of leadership. *Courage Over Fear* shows us the way to navigate this moment and strive for something better."

—Chris Ward, California State Assembly Member and Chair of the California State Legislative LGBTQ Caucus

"*Courage Over Fear* is the kind of book we need right now—not just for executives, but for anyone who's ever had to lead in uncertain times. Kristen Kavanaugh brings the perspective of a Marine Corps officer who's been tested in both service and the corporate world, and together with Mike Randolph, she's created a practical, inspiring guide for leading with integrity when fear is loudest. This isn't just a leadership book—it's a call to step up."

—Jason Kander, Afghanistan veteran, humanitarian activist, and bestselling author of *Invisible Storm: A Soldier's Memoir of Politics and PTSD*

"This book is a lantern for those leading in the dark. With wisdom and heart, Kristen and Mike remind us that courage isn't the absence of fear—it's the practice of aligning with purpose, again and again. Their framework is both grounding and galvanizing, offering not just hope, but a path forward in these challenging times."
—Dr. Vijay Pendakur, bestselling author of *The Alchemy of Talent*

"HR leaders are the connective tissue of any organization—we sit at the intersection of people, performance, and culture. In a climate defined by disruption, *Courage Over Fear* shares a usable framework for developing the kind of leadership our organizations need: grounded, values-driven, and equipped to navigate uncertainty. This is a book that empowers leaders at every level to cultivate courageous teams and transform their organization from the inside out."
—Rachel Kaplan, CPO, Telecon

"Timely and transformative, this book is a masterclass in ethical conditioning—an essential training guide for sharpening a leader's decision-making and ability to navigate an increasingly complex world. A workout for your mind and spirit, as vital to your success as physical conditioning is for your body."
—Major General James Johnson, USAF (Ret.), Former Director, Integrated Resilience Office, Headquarters U.S. Air Force

"Innovation is rooted in human creativity and for that to flourish, it requires courageous leaders who are inspiring, collaborative, and kind. *Courage Over Fear* is a blueprint for leading with authenticity and agency, especially when you're building what's never been built before. If we want to solve big, urgent challenges—on Earth or beyond—we need more leaders willing to choose courage over fear. This book is a guide for exactly that."
—**Darby Dunn, Engineering and Operations Executive**

"Courage is the one thing most companies are missing, and the thing they need the most. In a world with more uncertainty due to politics, climate change, and AI, leaders who step up courageously will be the ones that thrive. This does not mean erasing or suppressing fear, but facing real risks head-on, staring them in the face, and acting with conviction to drive yourself and your community forward. *Courage Over Fear* inspires, provokes, and motivates those among us who are ready to rise to the challenge. If you were drawn to this book, chances are you are one of us."
—**Tatyana Mamut, co-founder and CEO, Wayfound**

amplify

an imprint of Amplify Publishing Group

www.amplifypublishinggroup.com

Courage Over Fear: Harness the Power of Agency to Lead in Uncertain Times

For more information, please contact:
Amplify Publishing, an imprint of Amplify Publishing Group
620 Herndon Parkway, Suite 220
Herndon, VA 20170
info@amplifypublishing.com

Library of Congress Control Number: 2025907545

CPSIA Code: PRV0825A

ISBN-13: 979-8-89138-461-3

Printed in the United States

For Wesley and Miles Kavanaugh
and Thomas and Eldon Randolph

So you never have to wonder
what we did to fight back

KRISTEN
KAVANAUGH

MIKE
RANDOLPH

COURAGE
OVER
FEAR

HARNESS THE POWER OF AGENCY
TO LEAD IN UNCERTAIN TIMES

amplify
an imprint of Amplify Publishing Group

CONTENTS

Introduction

"What just happened?" We found ourselves asking this question more often than we'd like to admit on our journey through the leadership ranks at Tesla, one of the world's most recognizable tech companies. (We also used much more colorful language in those moments of extreme frustration, but we'll keep it clean, for now.) We were often blindsided by hasty operational decisions and dumbfounded by the lack of consideration for how those decisions impacted our most valuable asset—our people.

Chances are, you've asked yourself this same question—*What just happened?*—as a leader. Maybe you, too, have felt the need to rein in your reaction, moderate your tone, or worse yet, hold back your thoughts and ideas at work when faced with situations that seem to defy all logic. We've been there—surviving in "Keep your job" mode, grappling with learned helplessness, and doing whatever it took to provide for our families while we struggled to help our teams find their way through the chaos and uncertainty.

After leaving Tesla, we found ourselves reckoning with the countless "WTF" moments that had defined our experiences. Those moments weren't just frustrating—they were also formative, leaving behind a mix of lessons and unresolved questions.

Our conversations inevitably drifted toward "would've, could've, should've." What if we would've acted differently? What if we could've seized opportunities we missed at the time? We should've summoned the courage to make different choices. Then would things have turned out differently?

There was a restlessness in these reflections—a sense of unfinished business that wouldn't let go. While we couldn't rewrite the past, one word kept rising to the surface as we revisited those pivotal moments: *agency*. At first, it felt abstract, but the more we examined it, the more it revealed itself as the invisible string connecting the choices we made—and the ones we didn't. Agency—the ability to make intentional decisions based on your values—was both a source of power and a glaring absence in the moments we wished had gone differently. It was the missing ingredient in the moments we regretted and the driving force behind the decisions we were proud of.

> **Tab This!**
>
> Agency is the ability to make intentional decisions based on your values.

Chances are, you've also found yourself asking this same question—*What just happened?*—a lot lately. We certainly have, especially when reflecting on the larger societal shifts happening around us. The United States is increasingly marked by uncertainty, with authoritarianism and divisive rhetoric on the rise, and fear-based leadership becoming the norm—rendering courageous, values-driven leaders less visible and less influential. In the aftermath of the 2024 election, figures like Donald Trump and Elon Musk—deeply flawed leaders whose character issues would have once been disqualifying—are upheld as models of executive success, even as they normalize the racist, sexist, homophobic, and xenophobic behaviors and rhetoric that now permeate our workplaces and communities at great cost. Fear and uncertainty are fueling a cultural shift where authoritarian leadership thrives. These same larger-than-life leaders with authoritarian tendencies rely on fear, control, and division, which create environments where control overshadows collaboration, and division erodes trust. This reliance on oppressive tactics, once only seen in repressive regimes, has seeped into the workplace, creating environments where fear is no longer just a response to uncertainty but the foundation of how leaders operate and teams are expected to function.

The uncertainty leaders face—marked by constant upheaval, paralyzed inaction, and missed opportunities—is pervasive across our workplaces and communities. Fear of the unknown is pushing leaders to abandon thoughtful decision-making and adopt reactionary, often harmful, behaviors they might once have rejected. As leaders grapple with their own responses to the fear of uncertainty, many have begun to wield fear as a tool to regain a sense of control. This shift has transformed fear from a personal reaction into a deliberate strategy—one that prioritizes power and control over trust and collaboration, further entrenching division both in the workplace and beyond.

We've felt it—the pull to withdraw, the temptation to tune out the noise, and the struggle to reconcile a sense of powerlessness as authoritarian figures gain influence, spreading anxiety and division throughout our communities. And it disturbed us so deeply, we realized we couldn't stand by and tolerate it. The toxicity became a call to action—a clear imperative to lead, reclaim our agency, and create a better way forward.

And then it clicked: the key to overcoming fear and uncertainty wasn't just understanding agency—it was about choosing courage over fear. *Choosing courage over fear* to act when the stakes were high, *choosing courage over fear* to trust our instincts in uncertain times, and *choosing courage over fear* to lead in ways that aligned with our values. We realized it wasn't just agency that defined those moments; it was also choosing *courage over fear* to exercise our agency that shaped our impact—on our teams, our communities, and ourselves.

The Agency Loop

It became clear that addressing these challenges required more than just individual reflection—it needed collective action. That's why we founded The Agency Initiative—an organizational effectiveness and leadership development firm—to call forth courage in leaders, help them step into their agency, and create workplaces and communities where people thrive. We believe that by empowering leaders to embrace courage and reject fear-based, authoritarian approaches, those "What just happened?" and "WTF" moments can transform into something better—opportunities for growth, connection, and impact.

Through our consulting work with our clients, we discovered that having courage alone isn't enough. Courageous leadership—rooted in authenticity, agency, and a commitment to growth—is the key to cutting through the tension of these moments, transforming chaos into clarity, and fostering a more effective and fulfilling leadership experience. In an era marked by unprecedented uncertainty, courageous leadership is not just a skill but a necessity—a powerful antidote to the fears and disruptions shaping our workplaces and communities. It equips leaders to stand firm against the rise of fear-based rhetoric, navigate divisive environments with integrity, and create spaces where collaboration and inclusivity thrive. In doing so, courageous leadership offers a path forward that inspires trust, resilience, and curiosity, empowering us to meet the challenges of today's world head-on.

Specifically, based on our work at The Agency Initiative, we developed The Agency Loop to provide leaders with a structured framework for practicing courageous leadership. Its three phases—authenticity, agency, and growth—guide leaders through critical moments in their leadership journey:

- Authenticity phase: Where you align who you are with how you show up in the world
- Agency phase: Where you make intentional decisions based on your values
- Growth phase: Where you learn, adapt, and evolve through your experiences

You'll learn more about The Agency Loop and its connection back to courageous leadership throughout the book. You'll also get our perspectives, experiences, and the hard-earned lessons we've learned in anecdotes we call "Moments That Mattered." Finally, you'll get to walk through case studies to help you lead courageously in the face of three of today's most pressing challenges: the deprioritization of diversity, equity, and inclusion (DEI); political and social polarization; and rapid rise of innovation in the workplace.

The Future of Leadership Is Courageous

As we began writing, we found ourselves envisioning the kind of future we want to create—a future that goes beyond merely surviving today's challenges. We've already mentioned we will discuss fear, uncertainty, polarization, and the rise of authoritarianism—topics that can feel heavy and discouraging. That's why it was essential for us to anchor on a vision of hope, something that pulls us out of the doom and gloom and toward a future worth striving for.

Inspired by our mutual love for sci-fi nerd culture, we couldn't help but think of the *Star Wars* versus *Star Trek* debate. *Star Wars* often centers on existential conflicts between light and dark, good versus evil, with powerful displays of courage against oppressive systems. While these stories of resistance have their place, especially now, we envision a different kind of courage leading to a different kind of future—a *Star Trek* future. The iconic sci-fi franchise depicts a future where humanity has overcome war, poverty, and division to explore the galaxy as part of a united Federation. *Star Trek* imagines a future built on curiosity, exploration, and diplomacy—a vision where courageous leadership unites diverse people and ideas to solve problems and build a better universe.

A *Star Trek* future is not without conflict, but it's grounded in a fundamental belief that discovery and collaboration—guided by integrity and a shared purpose—are the keys to overcoming challenges and creating a thriving, connected world. In this future, courage isn't about conquering enemies—it's about building connections, uniting humanity, and charting a path toward shared purpose, opportunity, and possibility.

With this book, we are exercising our own agency in service of taking one step toward a *Star Trek* future. We're working toward a future where courageous, values-driven leadership is the norm, where diversity is celebrated as a strength, and where leaders are empowered to create workplaces grounded in trust, resilience, and curiosity. It's an ambitious vision, but one we deeply believe in. We're thrilled to have you join us as we shape a future where every leader, regardless of title, feels empowered to make a meaningful difference.

This book isn't just about recognizing the challenges leaders face—it's about equipping you with the tools to face them head-on. In the chapters ahead, you'll discover practical strategies, real-world examples, and actionable steps to cultivate courageous leadership. From navigating workplace tensions to fostering inclusive environments and leading through uncertainty, each chapter will guide you in applying authenticity, agency, and growth to create meaningful change in your organization and beyond.

This book is for anyone striving to lead with purpose: business leaders navigating toxic work cultures, community leaders working to make an impact, and teams building courageous, values-driven organizations. It's for new managers, experienced leaders, and anyone feeling silenced or isolated in the face of today's challenges. Whether you're dreaming of a better workplace, seeking to inspire your team, or working toward a future led by compassion and purpose, this book offers the tools and guidance to help you lead with courage over fear.

While many leadership books focus on the experiences and perspectives of CEOs—stories from the top—this book is different. We're not offering advice from those already in the C-suite, often disconnected from the realities of frontline leadership. Instead, this book is written by leaders who have been in the thick of it: navigating toxic work cultures, juggling impossible expectations, and doing everything they can to support their teams while simply trying to survive. It's for those on the front lines, working to make a difference right where they are, even when the odds feel stacked against them.

Ultimately, this book is our call to action for you—leaders ready to step up, embrace courage, and inspire change. It's not just about recognizing the challenges you face; it's about equipping you with the tools to confront them head-on. Together, we can build a community of courageous, values-driven leaders who transform their workplaces and the world around them. As you read, we invite you to envision the kind of leader you want to be and the future you want to create—because courageous leadership isn't just about navigating today's uncertainty; it's also about shaping tomorrow's opportunities.

HOW TO USE
THIS BOOK

How to Use This Book

You can't put your leadership on autopilot. Think of *Courage Over Fear* as a navigation tool to keep by your side on your leadership journey. Here are some tips and best practices for getting the most out of this book.

Read the Whole Thing

There is something in this book for everyone. Whether you're a new manager, an experienced leader, or someone looking to make a difference, you'll find ideas and tools to support your journey. To get the most out of it, we recommend reading it in order the first time. Here's an overview so you know what to expect.

Part 1 lays the foundation by presenting the case for courage and introducing The Agency Loop. We examine the corporate environment within the broader context of society, highlighting the uncertainty that permeates both. This section makes the argument for courageous leadership and provides you with a practical, proven framework for navigating uncertainty. The Agency Loop equips you to make courageous decisions faster, achieve better outcomes, and stay aligned with your values.

Part 2 builds on the foundation as both a call to action and an optional guide to practice. It explores the future of our workplaces and communities, focusing on how leadership evolves to meet new challenges. Leadership isn't just a title—it's an action rooted in purpose and the drive to create meaningful impact. We examine three critical uncertainties—the deprioritization of DEI; political and social polarization; and the rapid rise of innovation—that we believe are profoundly shaping workplaces today. This section invites you to join us in leading courageously through these complexities.

The Additional Resources section at the end of the book is designed to help you put the concepts from The Agency Loop into practice. It includes tools, exercises, and case studies that will deepen your understanding and support you as you apply the principles of courageous leadership to real-world challenges. As you progress through the book, use these resources to reflect on the material, practice new strategies, and integrate them into your leadership journey. This section serves as a guide to ensure that your growth continues beyond the pages of the book and into your daily leadership practice.

Jot Down Your Moments That Matter

We share our personal stories in sections we call Moments That Mattered. These are pivotal moments—the successes, the challenges, and the lessons we learned along the way—that shaped our understanding of leadership. These are the experiences where our learning happened, moments that tested us, changed us, shifted our career paths, and guided us toward the practices we share in this book. Some of these stories may sound familiar to your own experiences, bringing back memories and the emotions that came with them. As you read, you may find yourself recalling some of the most defining moments from your own career. Don't let those reflections pass by. This is an opportunity to explore those memories with curiosity rather than judgment—to write them down in the margins and revisit them later. You can share them with us at www.agency-initiative.com and let us know how they shaped your values, your choices, and the way you lead today.

In asking you to reflect, we're inviting you to consider the lessons those moments hold for you now and to apply the new perspectives we offer throughout this book. Think about how these experiences have influenced your approach to leadership, the assumptions you hold, and the ways you respond in challenging situations. Moments That Matter are about learning and growth, for us and for you. We hope these stories will encourage you to embrace your own pivotal moments as powerful teachers on your journey to becoming a courageous leader.

Make It Matter

Courage grows through small, intentional actions. Every chapter ends with a "Make It Matter" section—your opportunity to pause, reflect, and take action. These questions are designed to help you connect the chapter's ideas to your own leadership journey. Whether you're reflecting on a Moment That Mattered, exploring your values, or planning your next courageous step, this is your chance to make what you've read real. For further support in applying these ideas, don't forget to explore the Additional Resources section at the end of the book, where you'll find tools, exercises, and case studies to deepen your practice and guide your next steps.

Get to Know Taylor and Justin

We have great stories, and you'll see that we share them when we can, but we also believe you can learn from a well-developed narrative. We created Taylor and Justin as fictional composite characters for our case studies to represent our Everyman-ager. In the case studies, they will help demonstrate the intricacies of the loop in a way you can learn from their interactions and stories from start to finish. There are no stereotypes here. We both identify with parts of each character and their journey. We hope you do too.

Tag the Sections That Resonate with You

We love a good tabbed book. Grab some tabs and mark the sections that resonate with you. Underline the parts that you want to share with others. Write your own notes and comments in the margins. Do whatever you need to do to turn this thing into something that works for you when you need it most. Revisit sections when you feel like you are stuck. We know you are strapped for time. Make finding the important information as easy as possible in the moments you need it most. Throughout your journey you will use some sections more than others. That's the point. This book meets you where you are, no matter your place on your journey.

Keep It on Your Desk

A good tool is never too far out of reach. Keep it close to you. You'll be more inclined to pick it up when you have questions or need a quick refresher.

Share It with Your Team

Bring your team into the loop. Share the book with them and start to create some organizational language around the concepts in the book. Buy it as a team development tool and work together to operationalize the work within your organization. Include them along your journey and invite them to start their own. To find team development resources like discussion guides, visit our website at www.agency-initiative.com.

Recommend It to Colleagues and Professional Organizations

Pass it on. The book is a catalyst for courageous leadership. Share it with colleagues and professional circles to ignite curiosity, build a community, and start a movement toward a more courageous way of leading.

Embody It—Choose Courage Over Fear and Run the Loop

Courageous leadership is a daily practice. The real impact of The Agency Loop lies not just in understanding these principles but in embodying them. Start with small, intentional actions—show up with the intention to build trust, resilience, and curiosity in each interaction—and watch as these values shape your journey and impact as a leader.

PART 1

COURAGEOUS LEADERSHIP AND THE AGENCY LOOP

The pressure on leaders today has never been greater. Organizations demand leaders who can navigate complexity, inspire innovation, and foster collaboration. Yet many fall into the trap of control—gripping tighter, shutting down dissent, and prioritizing authority over authenticity. While these tactics may offer the illusion of stability, they erode trust, stifle creativity, and undermine thriving workplaces.

We've been there and know the feelings all too well. In moments of uncertainty and fear, we saw how easy it was to default to control—and the damaging ripple effects that followed. But we also experienced something different: moments when courage prevailed over fear and enabled us to lead with clarity and purpose. These weren't accidental; they came from consciously acting in alignment with our values, even when it was uncomfortable.

True leadership requires courage. It's not about control—it's about connection and intentional action. Courageous leaders foster trust, resilience, and curiosity by creating spaces where diverse perspectives are welcomed, innovation flourishes, and teams thrive. Courageous leadership isn't a onetime act; it's a daily practice—a journey of reflection, action, and growth.

This is where The Agency Loop comes in. Designed to cultivate courageous, values-driven leadership, it's a continuous cycle of authenticity, agency, and growth. Each phase addresses a different challenge: reconnecting with your values, making intentional decisions, or learning from experience. It's not a linear path, but you can picture it as an expanding spiral, fueled by accumulating courage—reinforcing trust, resilience, and curiosity, three essential values in uncertain times.

Part 1 sets the stage for this journey. We'll begin with courage and its archnemesis—fear. Each subsequent chapter delves into a phase of the loop, with our real-world examples we call Moments That Mattered that show how courage grows incrementally, one intentional decision at a time. By the end, you'll have the tools to run the loop and lead with authenticity, embrace agency, and foster meaningful growth for yourself and your teams.

COURAGE
OVER FEAR

CHAPTER 1

Courageous Leadership

Courageous leadership isn't always about heroics or grand gestures. Sure, corporate life can feel like a battlefield, but here, courage isn't about dodging explosions—it's about everyday choices that make life better. It's about being vulnerable enough to admit you don't have all the answers, yet resilient enough to inspire others through your actions during tough times. Courageous leaders create spaces where people feel safe to take risks and speak up, all while navigating tension with integrity and purpose.

Kristen's Moment That Mattered: The Corporate Battlefield

I've seen both sides—the battlefield heroics that save lives across borders and the decisions that change lives in corporate spaces across cultures. But let's be clear: corporate life isn't war. So why do corporate leaders feel the weight of a battlefield on their shoulders and pass that pressure on to their teams, especially in a globalized world where one decision can ripple across continents? Courageous leaders know the stakes are high, but they also know how to keep their teams grounded in trust and collaboration, not fear and anxiety. Just as I learned during my time as a Marine Corps officer, leading with courage, now in corporate spaces, means uniting people under shared values, even when external forces threaten to divide us.

It was 2020, nearly a year into the pandemic, and my anxiety was real. I was Tesla's Director of Inclusion, Talent, and Learning, the first to take up this configuration of the role. As part of my unofficial duties, I would wake up every morning, check Twitter and the newsfeed to see what our CEO had tweeted or which articles had been published that could send the day off the rails, and brace for what I'd be virtually walking into at work. Most days, the tweets were innocuous, mostly obnoxious, but some days they came in hot, hit hard, and blew a hole in my team's efforts. One day, he tweeted a midnight meme mocking the use of gender pronouns. No context. Nothing else. Short. Simple. And a total bomb.

Anger, then fear, then dread were my first reactions. What was I going to face when I logged in to my email? The backlash was swift and fierce. Internally, employees were reeling. Externally, media outlets were having a field day. Organizations we had partnered with were questioning our commitment to the LGBTQ+ community—my community. It was another day on the corporate battlefield. And I had to choose courage over avoidance.

This one was personal. As a member of the queer community, I knew that pronouns could mean the difference between safety and vulnerability—life and death—for some of us. Speaking up in cases like this often felt like stepping into a minefield. Not in the military sense, where hierarchy and tradition dominate and advocating for change can feel dangerous, even when lives are at stake. At Tesla, the stakes were different yet daunting—challenging the tweeting habits of one of the world's richest and most influential men came with its own set of risks. I had to have the courage to wade into the metaphorical no man's land between him, the tweet, the public, and our employees.

My team was bombarded with questions and outrage. The hard truth was we couldn't control the personal tweets. That made me feel powerless in those moments. But I could control how I showed up, and that realization became a model for my team. I had to be resilient, staying grounded and focusing on what I could control for those who mattered most—our employees, especially the transgender members of our teams.

My team listened to our employees' pain and outrage. Some of them handed us our asses, as if we had tweeted that nonsense. Still, we didn't take it personally. We held space for their emotions, not rushing to silence them but leaning into their experiences and learning.

We asked ourselves hard questions: If we can't stop the tweets, what can we do to better support our LGBTQ+ employees? How do we demonstrate our commitment in action? How could we ensure that action benefited the most people? These reflections sparked new initiatives—not just to recover from the crisis but to enshrine our commitment in policy and offerings. We partnered more closely with our community of transgender employees to ensure they felt safe and included. We introduced specialized, affirming health-care benefits and organized listening and learning sessions to help our employees understand the trans experience and the important role of pronouns. Our ideas became reality, transforming the employee experience for the better. Our focus was on what I could influence and control at my level, keeping the momentum on the inclusive culture we were building overall.

I knew there would be more tweets, more crises, but something about this moment felt different. Looking back, I recognize that this was the turning point—a moment when I began to sense, perhaps subconsciously, that our leadership was starting to retreat from our diversity and inclusion commitments. Though it wasn't spoken or explicitly tweeted, I felt a shift in the metaphorical "Force." I knew it meant making a personal commitment to courage, no matter what tweet bombs were dropped.

This experience showed me that courageous leadership isn't about avoiding conflict; it's about facing it, even as the ground beneath us begins to shift. The challenges ahead would only get harder, but this moment deepened our resolve to stand firm in our values, preparing us for the rising tide against DEI that we would soon confront.

Courageous leadership isn't about making bold moves or sweeping decisions—it's about showing up in the trenches, grounded in values, when the stakes are highest. This moment on the corporate battlefield crystallized that truth for me. It also left me asking a deeper question: What exactly is courage? Before we can explore how it shapes leadership, we must define it—understanding not only what it is but also what it requires from us as individuals first, then as leaders.

Courage Defined

To us, courage is the resolve to face fear or uncertainty, guided by care for what truly matters. Let's break that down a bit. In times of change, when the path forward is unclear and the stakes feel high, fear and uncertainty challenge us to make tough choices. At its core, true courage is the inner strength to show up fully, to speak openly and honestly about who we are, and to lead with authenticity.

Courage is the resolve to face fear or uncertainty,
guided by care for what truly matters.

Courage isn't the absence of fear. In fact, fear is a central component of courage. Now fear can, and in many instances does, come in many different forms. It shows up in subtle and powerful ways, influencing how we respond to challenges and uncertainty. Understanding these different forms of fear allows us to recognize it, name it, and then take action to move through it. Let's take a look at a few that we often see show up with our clients.

- Fear of uncertainty. This is the fear of the unknown—What happens next? How will this unfold? When the path forward isn't clear, it's tempting to cling to the familiar, even if it's holding us back.
- Fear of loss. This fear is rooted in the possibility of losing something important—security, status, relationships, or identity. It forces us to confront the uncomfortable question: What if this costs me more than I'm willing to give?
- Fear of change. This fear comes from the discomfort of leaving behind the familiar and stepping into the unknown—What if this change disrupts what's working and makes things worse? What if I can't adapt?
- Fear of failure. This fear stems from the uncertainty of outcomes—What if we don't succeed? What if we let others down or damage our reputation? In leadership,

this can show up as hesitation to take risks, avoidance of tough decisions, or perfectionism that stifles progress.

- Fear of judgment. This form of fear comes from worrying about how others perceive us—What if they don't approve? What if I stand out in a way that invites ridicule or rejection?

Throughout the rest of the book, we will address how some of these fears show up for us in the workplace and how to use The Agency Loop to enlist courage over fear.

Finally, as Brené Brown reminds us in *I Thought It Was Just Me (But It Isn't)*, "Courage is a heart word. The root of courage is *cor*—the Latin word for heart."[1] Courage, she explains, requires the inner strength and commitment to show up honestly and vulnerably, to speak openly about who we are and what matters most to us—good or bad. That's why we emphasize *care for what truly matters* in our definition of courage. At its core, courage is about leading with heart and caring for people—it's about showing up for what's worth fighting for.

When leaders embrace this deeper sense of courage, they can face the unknown with resilience, make values-driven decisions, and inspire those around them. This chapter explores what it means to lead courageously in the face of fear and uncertainty—why it's essential, how it's cultivated, and how it can transform the challenges we face into opportunities for growth.

The Inner and Outer Game

When we think about courage in the workplace, we often focus on what we are *doing*—bold acts like standing up in a room full of people or making a tough decision under pressure. But there's another side to courage: *being*. Courageous leadership isn't just about the visible actions we take—it's about who we are when we show up in the Moments That Matter. Drawing from executive coach and founder of Coaching from Essence, Robert Ellis, we agree that leaders must master both their inner and outer games to truly step into courageous leadership. Ellis describes the inner and outer game this way:

- Inner game: This is your mindset, values, emotional resilience, and authenticity—how you handle challenges internally. (Who are you going to be?)
- Outer game: These are the actions you take—leading decisively, taking risks, and making choices that align with your inner values. (What are you going to do?)[2]

When we think about courage, most of us focus heavily on the outer game, with questions like, "What's the next step? What actions should I take?" And while that's valid—what we do matters—the inner game is often overlooked. It's easy to replay our actions in our heads, but it's much harder to engage courageously with our mindset, values, and emotions during those moments. Yet it's this willingness to reflect deeply on who we are that leads to real transformation as leaders. True courage is not only about taking bold actions. It's about examining ourselves honestly and choosing to grow from within.

In our experience, focusing on the outer game and courageous acts can only take us so far. We can make bold decisions, take risks, and get things done, but without a strong sense of who we are—our being—those actions may not fully align with our core values. The real shift happens when we work on the inner game, when we reflect deeply on our values and sense of purpose. Once our *being* is clear and aligned, our *doing*—our actions—naturally follows, and with far greater impact.

It's work on the inner game that can help leaders make major gains. The inner game is the foundation of courageous leadership. It's the internal work of shaping our mindset, grounding ourselves in our values, and building the emotional resilience necessary to navigate challenges with integrity. Developing this inner game means facing our own fears, examining our intentions, and committing to lead from a place of authenticity, even when the path is uncertain. It's about understanding who we are at our core—our strengths, limitations, and the beliefs that drive us. When leaders invest in this inner work, they cultivate a courage that enables them to make tough decisions and take meaningful action that reflects their true values. With a strong inner game, our outer actions align naturally with our purpose, allowing us to lead not only decisively but with unwavering conviction.

Building a strong inner game is what allows leaders to show up courageously, even in the face of fear and uncertainty. Courageous leadership is often about small, consistent actions that align with our core values. This is where the idea of "small acts of courage" comes in. Rather than aiming for sweeping changes, we can focus on making progress one small step at a time.

Small Acts of Courage

As leadership scholar and psychologist Manfred F. R. Kets de Vries says, "Perhaps the best way to think of courage is to treat it as a muscle. Some people are born with better muscles than others, but everyone can improve their muscles through training and practice."[3] Leadership offers countless opportunities to work that muscle through small, everyday acts. It's not just in moments of crisis or high-stakes decision-making that courage reveals itself—though those moments certainly matter. Often, it's in the quieter, less glamorous moments when no one is watching that leadership courage is truly tested and strengthened.

Courageous acts don't need to be grand. They can be as simple as speaking up in a difficult conversation, offering a dissenting opinion, or stepping back to listen when you feel the impulse to react. These seemingly small moments can have a profound impact on the people around you, and they compound over time to shape who you are as a leader.

Kristen's Moment That Mattered: The 5 Percent Shift

One of the most transformative ideas I've encountered came from my coach: "What would it look like to be 5 percent more courageous?" Five percent seemed doable. It wasn't about making sweeping changes or having all the answers. It was about finding small moments to push myself—just a little further—when it really counted.

That 5 percent approach became a lifeline—a manageable way to step up, even when everything around me felt overwhelming. It wasn't about having the perfect words or the ultimate solution; it was about leaning in when the stakes were high and fear was present. And then, the world shifted dramatically.

George Floyd's murder had sparked a nationwide racial reckoning, and companies everywhere were scrambling to respond. I had just returned from parental leave, where my newborn had spent forty-four days in the NICU. The pandemic was raging, and I was exhausted.

Upon my return, I was asked to step back into my role as head of diversity and inclusion. I was in the process of rebuilding the organization from the ground up after the departure of our first head of D&I, who had done everything in her power to gain traction for the work, despite being constantly pulled in a million directions by her dual role as an HR executive. Now with only two of us left to carry the D&I work, the task ahead felt massive. On top of that, I was asked to take on four additional organizations: talent management, performance management, customer learning, and employee learning and development, a set of functions that had been leaderless, ironically, since the day I started parental leave. To add to the complexity, I had a new boss whom I had started reporting to a few weeks before I started parental leave. I was in survival mode, both at work and at home.

And now, in this high-pressure moment in the wake of George Floyd's murder, I was being looked to for answers—for leadership in a time of crisis. But I didn't have all the answers. What I did know was that we needed to approach the situation with authenticity. Yet what did "authentic" even mean for us as a company so early into our D&I journey?

I watched other companies change their social media profile pictures, put out CEO statements, and make promises. Much of it was performative, and employees were quick to call them out. We were struggling with our own response. Multiple ideas were on the table. One of the first included a shocking proposal—fly a Black Lives Matter flag at our factory.

My heart sank. We had no business proclaiming such a bold stance, especially given the number of employment lawsuits we were facing and the lingering, unresolved questions in the public domain about how we were treating our Black employees. These issues cast a shadow over our credibility, and the scrutiny from both inside and outside the company underscored the urgent need to rebuild trust and integrity within our organization. Flying a BLM flag, at that factory, at that moment, was not a good idea.

It would be performative—exactly the kind of empty gesture that was getting called out, rightfully so, by employees at other companies. My boss, who also identified as Black, was open to the idea, and I understood where she was coming from. It would be a bold statement, albeit an aspirationally bold statement, that I desperately wanted to be true. I wanted us to be in a position where we could genuinely emphasize our support for the Black community, but I also like to live in reality. We weren't there yet. We weren't even close.

This was within my first month back, tensions were high, and emotions—my own included—were even higher. I knew I had to push back, but how? That's when I remembered my coach's advice: "What would it look like to be 5 percent more courageous?"

I didn't need to solve the entire problem in one conversation. I just needed to take a small step. I needed to speak up—not to judge, not to criticize, but to open the conversation and stay curious.

With my heart in my throat, I voiced my concern. I explained that flying the flag wouldn't be authentic, given the current state of our workplace culture. To my relief, my boss agreed. She understood that we needed to approach this differently. Instead of flying the flag or a whole host of other performative acts, she decided to release a deeply personal statement placing a stake in the ground on her position and setting the tone for how she would lead a cultural shift within the company.[4] Tactically, we focused internally on listening to understand our employees. We created spaces for honest conversations, helping our broader workforce understand the pain that their colleagues were feeling. These weren't profound actions. But they were authentic to where we were on our D&I journey.

This experience taught me that courage doesn't require sweeping changes or fearless confidence—it begins with small, intentional steps. That 5 percent shift was enough to spark progress, even in the face of overwhelming fear and uncertainty. And it's in these small acts of courage, repeated over time, that the foundation of courageous leadership is built.

This experience reinforced a profound truth about leadership: courage isn't about eliminating fear but learning to navigate it. It's not about extravagant effort or sweeping fixes—it's about small, intentional steps that align with your values, even when fear or uncertainty threatens to hold you back. These moments of courage, however small, define how leaders show up in the most challenging times.

Courageous leadership builds on this foundation. At its core, it's about recognizing fear not as a barrier but as an invitation to act with courage. In the next section, we'll explore what it truly means to lead courageously, why it's essential in today's world, and how it transforms challenges into opportunities for growth.

Courageous Leadership

At the heart of leadership lies a paradox: courage can't exist without fear, and growth can't happen without uncertainty—yet as humans, we try to avoid fear and uncertainty like the plague. Courage is sparked by the presence of fear—it pushes us to dig deeper, to face what scares us, and to step forward anyway.

As Frank Herbert wrote in *Dune*, the Litany Against Fear states, "Fear is the mind-killer."[5] It's the force that paralyzes us, that clouds our judgment, and that prevents us from acting in alignment with our values. But courage isn't about fearlessness—it's about vulnerability and the ability to recognize fear, doubt, or uncertainty and choose to act anyway.

We see fear as the initiator of courage—a signal that we're standing at the edge of growth.

Courage in leadership means acknowledging the fear that comes with uncertainty and choosing to lead through it. Growth is only possible when we step into the unknown, into spaces that feel uncomfortable and uncharted. Fear and uncertainty are not obstacles to overcome; they are the conditions that call forth our courage and fuel our growth.

Herbert captures this well as the Litany continues: "I will face my fear. I will permit it to pass over me and through me."[6]

Specifically, courageous leadership is your ability to act *based on your values* in the face of fear. Courageous leaders believe in the power of these qualities and embody them in their actions. It's about leading with heart, staying connected to your values when things get tough, and having the courage to take action in uncertain times. Leadership isn't about wielding power; it's about being authentic, trustworthy, and unwavering in your commitment to lead others.

Values of a Courageous Leader: Trust, Resilience, and Curiosity

Courageous leadership is grounded in core values that guide leaders to navigate challenges with integrity and purpose. These values are not just guiding principles—they are practical tools that help leaders think, act, and lead with intention. Serving as anchors, they keep leaders grounded during times of uncertainty and adversity, enabling them to inspire trust and empower their teams.

While every leader brings their own unique set of values, shaped by their experiences and beliefs, we believe three core values define courageous leadership: trust, resilience, and curiosity. These foundational values are essential for navigating uncertainty, fostering collaboration, and driving meaningful growth. That said, they do not exist in isolation. Values like empathy, initiative, integrity, and dependability are important and contribute to a well-rounded leadership approach. For this framework, however, we'll focus on trust, resilience, and curiosity as the essential pillars that empower leaders to meet the demands of an ever-changing world with courage and purpose.

Balancing how you cultivate these qualities within yourself (inner game) with how you demonstrate them in your interactions (outer game) is key to courageous leadership. The inner game fosters authenticity and personal growth, while the outer game builds trust, resilience, and curiosity within teams, organizations, and communities.

When leaders demonstrate trustworthiness—by being transparent, reliable, and consistent—they create a sense of psychological safety for their teams. This safety allows individuals to share ideas, admit mistakes, and take risks without fear of judgment or retaliation. Trust counters the paralyzing effects of fear by fostering open communication and collaboration, empowering teams to move forward, even when the path ahead is unclear. At the same time, trust requires leaders to trust themselves, to have the confidence to make decisions, and to stand firm in their values. When that self-trust is reflected in their actions, it strengthens the trust others have in them, creating a powerful cycle of trust that extends beyond the individual leader to the entire team.

Resilience is the ability to adapt and recover in the face of challenges, and it's critical for navigating the high-stakes moments that define courageous leadership. Resilient leaders view setbacks as opportunities for growth, maintaining composure and focus even under pressure. This steadiness inspires confidence in others, enabling teams to weather difficult situations and emerge stronger. Resilience also equips leaders to handle criticism or failure without losing sight of their goals, demonstrating the strength to persevere and lead by example. At the core, resilience requires leaders to maintain their self-belief and emotional balance, even when external circumstances are challenging. When leaders model this inner strength through their actions, it creates a foundation of resilience within the team, encouraging them to stay focused and keep moving forward despite the obstacles they face.

Curiosity challenges the status quo and opens the door to growth, even in difficult circumstances. Courageous leaders use curiosity to seek out diverse perspectives, explore innovative solutions, and ask questions that deepen understanding. By approaching adversity with curiosity, leaders transform challenges into opportunities to learn and grow. This mindset not only drives creativity but helps leaders connect with their teams, fostering collaboration and innovation in uncertain times. Curiosity begins with introspective curiosity—taking the time to reflect on our own assumptions, biases, and understanding. This self-awareness enables leaders to ask better questions, seek alternative viewpoints, and create an open space for growth. When this internal curiosity is expressed externally, it fosters an environment of exploration and discovery, encouraging teams to embrace change and innovate together.

Table 1.1. Inner and Outer Game Values. Let's explore how these three core values manifest in both the inner and outer games of courageous leadership.

Trust: Belief in yourself and inspiring confidence through integrity and consistency	Inner Game: Self-Trust • Confidence in your own decisions and abilities, built through alignment with your values and consistent follow-through on commitments to yourself • Example: Trusting your judgment when faced with uncertainty
	Outer Game: Trustworthiness • Earning the confidence of others through reliability, honesty, and consistent actions • Example: Being transparent and dependable in your leadership to build confidence within your team
Resilience: The ability to adapt and bounce back from challenges	Inner Game: Personal Resilience • Your ability to bounce back from setbacks and navigate challenges with emotional stability and adaptability • Example: Learning from personal failure and maintaining focus despite adversity
	Outer Game: Collective Resilience • Creating environments that foster adaptability and recovery for others • Example: Supporting your team through a crisis by maintaining clear communication and providing resources
Curiosity: Openness to self-discovery and exploring others' perspectives	Inner Game: Introspective Curiosity • Openness to learning, self-reflection, and exploring your own thoughts, beliefs, and behaviors • Example: Reflecting on why you reacted a certain way in a tough conversation and seeking to understand yourself better
	Outer Game: Empathetic Curiosity • Engaging with others' perspectives and exploring new ideas to foster connection and innovation • Example: Asking thoughtful questions in a team discussion to uncover creative solutions

Trust, resilience, and curiosity aren't just stand-alone qualities—they are deeply interconnected in courageous leadership. Together, these values not only define courageous leadership—they drive the ability to lead with authenticity, make intentional decisions, and inspire others to embrace change. In uncertain times, these values are what empower leaders to transform challenges into opportunities, helping them lead with clarity, purpose, and the confidence to face whatever lies ahead. When leaders embrace these values, they model the kind of courage that inspires others, turning moments of fear or uncertainty into opportunities for transformation.

A Counterbalance to Fear-Based Leadership

While trust, resilience, and curiosity are the hallmarks of values-based, courageous leadership, fear-based leadership stands in stark opposition, eroding these very values. Fear-based leaders prioritize control over trust, conformity over curiosity, and short-term survival over long-term resilience. Driven by insecurity or external pressures, they reject vulnerability and centralize decision-making, shutting out dissenting voices and innovation. This often leads to micromanagement, reactive choices, and toxic environments where employees feel undervalued and failure is punished. Instead of fostering growth, fear-based leadership extracts value from people, creating stress, burnout, and cultures where fear—not courage—determines the path forward.

Fear-based leadership thrives on control and avoidance, steering leaders away from the very tensions that could drive growth. But courageous leadership isn't just the absence of fear—it's the willingness to engage with discomfort, wrestle with uncertainty, and move through tension with intention. These moments, when our instincts signal that something isn't right, are not threats but invitations to step into leadership. We will delve deeper into fear and its connection to courageous leadership in part 2 of this book.

Table 1.2. Comparing and Contrasting the
Courageous Leader and Fear-Based Leader

	Outer Game What are they doing?	**Inner Game** Who are they being?
Courageous Leaders	• Build trust by creating open, transparent communication channels, listening actively, and following through on commitments • Cultivate resilience by encouraging adaptability in the face of change, modeling a positive response to setbacks, and supporting a growth-oriented mindset • Engage in curiosity by asking thoughtful questions, encouraging diverse perspectives, and fostering a culture where exploration and learning are valued	• Vulnerable • Self-compassionate • Decisive • Intentional • Appreciative • Adaptive
Fear-Based Leaders	• Micromanage and seek to control by limiting decision-making authority to themselves, closely overseeing tasks, and stifling employees' autonomy and innovation • Shift blame and punish by deflecting responsibility when mistakes occur, focusing on assigning fault rather than addressing root causes, and using punitive measures to maintain authority • Prioritize short-term success by focusing on immediate results at the expense of long-term stability, disregarding the well-being of employees, and pushing for unsustainable output to quickly meet targets	• Insecure • Domineering • Manipulative • Rigid • Reactive • Self-serving

Wrestling with Dissonance and Tension

Courageous leadership often shines brightest when we're faced with challenges that demand more from us—moments when opportunities or tensions push us to act with conviction. It's in these moments that our values are tested and strengthened. But what activates a person's courage? How do we recognize the moments that call us to step up, speak out, or stand firm?

Tension

Your body often knows something is amiss before your brain catches up. Your heart races and palms sweat—these physical signals tell you something important is unfolding. We call that experience *tension*. Tension is an emotional, mental, or physical experience that causes dissonance. In short, it's a feeling in your body—when your Spidey senses tingle. These feelings signal to leaders that something doesn't feel quite right. It's that internal voice, the one that makes you pause and question, "What just happened?" or "Why does this feel wrong?"

Dissonance

Tension is a reaction to a metaphorical disturbance in the "Force." We call that disturbance *dissonance*. Dissonance is a conflict between your values and your environment. It is the catalyst that brings out a leader's courage. It stokes fear. It demands attention, forces action, and tests a leader's ability to navigate fear and uncertainty.

Brené Brown captures dissonance perfectly in *Dare to Lead*. She says, "We all know what it feels like to walk outside our values. We all know what it feels like to stay silent and comfortable instead of voicing what we believe."[7] And she is right; we do know. So then why is it so damn hard to do something in the moment? Often, you don't fully grasp their significance in the heat of the moment. It's only through reflection that the weight and lessons of these moments become clear.

But not every moment that makes your palms sweat holds the same weight. Some moments have a greater impact than others. Identifying and reflecting on these moments is an opportunity to *stop, take a beat, and get curious*. It takes courage to admit when you were rigid, defensive, or overbearing. To recognize that the values you believed you were living out weren't the ones showing up in the moment. Or to confront the wounds that may perpetuate harmful behaviors. Real growth comes when you align your actions with your values. This is where humility and true leadership come into play.

Tab This!

Stop. Take a beat. Get curious.

This simple phrase serves as a mnemonic for self-regulation and emotional grounding. It means pausing your actions, taking intentional time to reflect deeply on the situation, and pushing yourself to ask tougher questions: *Who was I being in that moment? What values were at play when I made that decision? How did that impact who I am today?* This tool helps leaders pause, reflect, and realign their responses, fostering intentionality and curiosity over reactivity. In moments of tension or uncertainty, it promotes awareness and a shift toward courageous, values-driven leadership.

Sometimes dissonance doesn't just challenge you—it reveals you. These are the moments that leave a mark, the ones we call Moments That Mattered. Whether you recognize it right away or years later, these moments force you to look inward, to examine your values, identities, and beliefs against the pressures or conflicts in the environment around you.

This inward examination is where courage begins, and it drops you directly into The Agency Loop, specifically into the authenticity phase. Authenticity is about understanding who you are and aligning how you show up in the world with what truly matters to you. These moments, especially Moments That Matter, invite you to clarify your values, confront your discomfort, and make choices that reflect your truest self.

Enter The Agency Loop

Leaders need something to help them manage the dissonance and tension they feel as their values collide with their environment, enabling them to make decisions that stay true to those values. The Agency Loop provides a practical approach to help leaders recognize fear and manage how they respond when they face the next *What just happened?* moment. Its three phases—authenticity, agency, and growth—guide leaders through a repeatable way to stop, take a beat, and get curious about critical moments in their leadership journey:

- Authenticity: Your ability to align who you are with how you show up in the world
- Agency: Your ability to make intentional decisions based on your values

- Growth: Your ability to learn, adapt, and evolve through your experiences

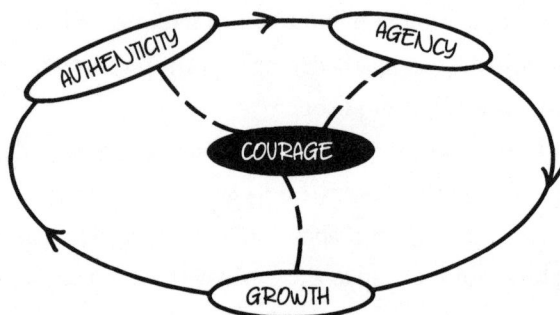

Courage is at the center of every phase of The Agency Loop, driving leaders to act with integrity and intention. Authenticity requires the courage to show up as your true self, even when it's uncomfortable or risky. It means rejecting conformity and standing firm in your values, regardless of external pressures. Agency demands the courage to make bold decisions in uncertain moments. And trusting yourself and your decisions, even when outcomes are unpredictable. It's acting with the confidence that your decisions reflect who you are. Growth is rooted in the courage to self-reflect—to take a look in the mirror and learn from failure, embrace feedback, and adapt without letting fear hold you back. This phase is where resilience is built, as leaders reflect on past actions and allow those lessons to guide their development.

The Agency Loop isn't just a concept—it's a practice. It offers leaders a way to reflect on their decisions, understand the impact of those decisions, and evolve as they face new challenges. It's called a "loop" because it's not linear; there's no endpoint, only cycles that build on each other, like the shape of a spiral, fueled by your courage with each pass. With this framework, leaders don't just survive moments of tension—they thrive, growing stronger and more capable each time they run the loop.

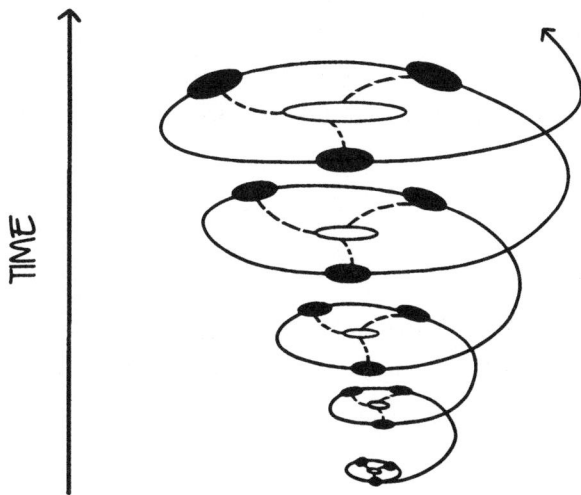

In the next three chapters, we will dive deep into each of the three phases of the loop, starting with the on-ramp, authenticity.

Make It Matter: Courageous Leadership

Use this short exercise to help you identify where you are and the next steps to take in your journey toward courageous leadership—because it only matters if you Make It Matter.

Courage: A Moment of Risk

Courage is not the absence of fear—it's taking action despite it. Every leader faces moments when they must decide whether to step forward or hold back. These moments of risk, big or small, define who we are as leaders.

In this exercise, you'll reflect on a time when you had to act with courage and explore how it shaped your leadership.

Think about a time when you had to show courage at work (or in your personal life). Maybe it was speaking up in a meeting, making a tough decision, or taking a risk when you weren't sure of the outcome.

Reflect

- What made that moment feel risky or uncertain?
- How did you move forward, and what did you learn from the experience?

Apply It Now—the 5 Percent More Courageous Approach

- How can you apply what you've learned to an upcoming situation where you might need to be courageous?

GET CURIOUS

CHAPTER 2

Authenticity

Authenticity is instrumental in courageous leadership. It's where your values, beliefs, and identity meet the reality of how you show up in the world. But authenticity in the workplace is often misunderstood. Popular phrases like "Bring your whole self to work" sound empowering, but they can create confusion about what authenticity truly means. Does it mean sharing everything about yourself? Expecting the workplace to embrace every aspect of who you are? Not quite.

Authenticity is about alignment—not oversharing. It's about bringing the parts of yourself that matter most to the work you do, while respecting the boundaries that allow you and your colleagues to thrive. In this chapter, we'll explore what it means to stop, take a beat, and get curious about how authenticity shows up in your leadership and why it's the critical starting point for The Agency Loop.

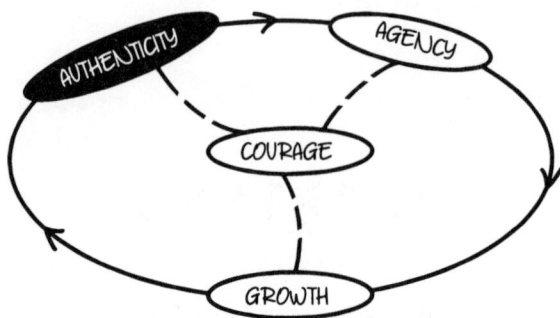

Kristen's Moment That Mattered: Bring Your Whole Self to Work

I said it many times. I wrote it into our strategy. It was our mantra—but I realized it was wrong. "Bringing your whole self to work" implies that everything is fair game, that all parts of who we are should show up in the workplace. While the sentiment is spot-on—we don't set aside our personal lives the second we badge into the building—the practical reality is different.

The truth is, we come to work to work. Work isn't our therapist, and it's not meant to handle every aspect of our personal lives. For some, work provides purpose and fulfillment; for others, it's just a paycheck. At the end of the day, the goal of work is to get the job done.

With that in mind, I've come to internalize a new mantra: *bring your authentic self to work*, along with a reminder that not every part of you belongs in the workplace. Your authentic self is still based on your identity, values, and beliefs. It influences your decision-making, but it also recognizes the need for professional boundaries. We don't have to bring everything to work—we just need to bring what matters to the work we do.

Authenticity Defined

When we talk about authenticity, we're talking about the alignment between who we are on the inside—our values, beliefs, and identity—and how we show up in the world. Within The Agency Loop, authenticity plays a crucial role. It's the on-ramp into the loop. It keeps us grounded, helping us navigate the complexities of leadership while staying true to our values. Authenticity isn't just where the process starts, and it's not the end goal. It's something we must continue to revisit and realign as we learn and grow—as we continue to loop.

> **Tab This!**
>
> Authenticity is the ability to align who you
> are with how you show up in the world.

That's because authenticity isn't static. It's fluid, changing as we learn, grow, and evolve. Management psychologist Karissa Thacker describes authenticity as the "process of inventing yourself" in her book *The Art of Authenticity*.[1] Who we are today isn't who we were five years ago, and that's expected. Courageous leadership requires us to reflect continuously on what we stand for, how our values are evolving, and how those values show up in our actions. Some parts of our authenticity are constant—our core values, the essence of who we are. But the way we express those values, especially in different roles or environments, can change.

As we grow and adapt, the challenge for leaders is ensuring that these shifts don't disconnect us from our essence. True authenticity requires us to embrace this fluidity while staying grounded in what matters most. It's not about being the same in every situation but about ensuring our actions remain rooted in who we are. Courageous leadership demands self-awareness and constant reflection: How are my values evolving? Am I still leading in a way that aligns with who I am today? Are there values that no longer serve me?

Authenticity, Values, and Identities

Authenticity isn't a leadership style or a set of characteristics someone can merely emulate.[2] Authenticity is a dynamic blend of the innate and the learned. The parts of us that feel most natural often represent our essence—like our temperament or instincts—while other aspects are shaped through experience and socialization—like cultural identities and social roles. This means that authenticity, in the leadership sense, isn't a style or just about declaring who we are; it's also about being willing to evolve and adapt, allowing our forms to shift in alignment with our core values.

The goal is always to ensure that, even as our environments change, the way we express ourselves remains rooted in who we are at our core. This requires ongoing self-compassion and reflection, as we navigate the delicate balance between being true to ourselves and adapting to the demands of leadership.

Authenticity is shaped by what we've experienced, what we believe, and the environments we navigate—but those same factors can also challenge our ability to stay authentic. Authenticity can present itself differently depending on context—especially between our personal and professional lives. At work, the pressures to conform or succeed may lead us to behave differently than we would in our personal lives, where societal norms and expectations from close relationships can dictate how we show up. Heard of "culture fit," anyone? How in the world can you be authentic when sometimes *fitting in* means *getting in*?

Values and Identity as the Anchors of Authenticity

Our values are the anchor of our authenticity—they define what matters most to us and provide a compass for how we engage with the world. When our actions align with these values, we feel genuine and build trust with others. However, misalignment—whether due to external pressures, fear, or uncertainty—creates tension, making it harder to lead authentically. Staying true to our values requires clarity and courage, especially in environments that challenge or test them. Authenticity isn't about being the same in every situation; it's about ensuring that, even as we adapt, our actions remain rooted in what we believe.

Authenticity is also deeply tied to our identities—how we see ourselves and how we are seen by others. Our identities are multifaceted, shaped by factors like culture, upbringing, and lived experiences. This is where the concept of intersectionality, first coined by Kimberlé Crenshaw, a pioneering scholar and writer on civil rights, becomes critical. Intersectionality recognizes that our identities don't exist in isolation; they overlap, creating unique experiences. For example, in the simplest terms, the experiences of a Black woman in leadership may differ from those of a white woman or a Black man, because her identity is shaped by both race and gender.[3]

These intersections often amplify the tension between belonging and self-expression, as leaders navigate environments that may only recognize or value parts of who they are. Understanding and embracing intersectionality allows leaders to honor their full complexity and bring a more inclusive perspective to how they lead. This complexity underscores the importance of alignment—ensuring that the way we show up reflects the whole of who we are, not just the parts the world finds easiest to accept.

Identity

Since our identities are multifaceted, they shape how we see the world and how the world sees us. To better understand the layers that make up who we are, we lean on Michael Hecht's Communication Theory of Identity (CTI). In his work, Hecht and Kaitlin Phillips lay out four key layers—personal identity, relational identity, communal identity, and enacted identity—that interact to shape our leadership and how we show up in the world.[4]

We chose CTI because leadership is, at its core, about communication—how we express our values, navigate relationships, and show up in different contexts. Unlike models that focus solely on psychology or sociology, CTI captures how identity is lived and negotiated in real time, making it a powerful tool for understanding authenticity in leadership. We use the *personal identity* portion of their model to help us explore the relationship between identity and authenticity.

At the core, personal identity reflects who we are at our essence—things like race, gender, ethnicity, and family background. These intrinsic dimensions of our identity shape how we navigate the world. But identity doesn't stop there. Other identities come from the choices we make, the roles we take on, and the commitments we embrace. Whether it's a title like manager, vice president, or mentor, or a role like mother, athlete, or marine, these identities are equally important. They reflect what we do, the environments we choose to be part of, and the ways in which we express our values.

CTI reminds us that identity, like authenticity, isn't static—it's fluid, shaped by our interactions, environments, and personal growth. To lead authentically, we must understand how these layers intersect, how they inform our leadership, and how we can stay true to ourselves while navigating the complexities of our roles. This ongoing self-awareness is essential for leaders to embrace authenticity, not just in our personal lives but in the way we lead and influence others.

For leaders, this can get complicated. These layers of identity can align harmoniously, but they can also create tension. A vice president who is also a mother may find herself balancing competing demands, while a marine turned executive might wrestle with how their military background shapes their leadership approach. These different identities—both intrinsic and acquired—influence how we lead, the values we hold dear, and the relationships we build.

Authenticity in leadership requires us to acknowledge and embrace all the layers of our identity. It's not about presenting one aspect of ourselves at the expense of others—it's about understanding how our multiple identities inform the way we show up. This means reflecting on the aspects of identity we choose to bring forward in different contexts, while also honoring the parts of ourselves that may remain in the background. True authenticity in leadership isn't about leaving certain identities at the door; it's about intentionally choosing how to present ourselves in ways that align with both our values and the demands of our roles.

Embracing these layers of identity isn't just about becoming more self-aware—it's about cultivating the courage to lead authentically. It's about having the strength to bring your authentic self into your leadership while balancing those identities in ways that empower you and those you lead. By doing so, we not only stay true to our values, but we also give others permission to do the same.

Alignment

These layers of identity are essential to who we are, but to lead authentically, we must align them with our actions and decisions. At the heart of authenticity is alignment—the harmony between our inner self (our values, beliefs, and identity) and our outer actions (how we show up and engage with others). This is where Robert Ellis's concepts of the inner game (our values, beliefs, and identity) and the outer game (our behaviors, actions, and decisions) come into play.[5] Authenticity thrives when these two are in sync. When our actions reflect our values and identities, we lead courageously. But when there's a disconnect—when our actions don't match our values or identities—dissonance and tension arise. We've all felt it—the self-doubt, frustration, or burnout that comes when who we are on the inside clashes with how we're showing up in the world.

This is why alignment matters—not just between our values and actions, but also between our inner clarity and how we're perceived by others. The inner game is about understanding who we are and what we stand for, while the outer game is about ensuring that our decisions and behaviors reflect that understanding. Bridging these two requires constant recalibration, especially in environments that challenge us to compromise. Leadership rooted in authenticity isn't about perfection—it's about having the courage to stay true to yourself while effectively engaging with the world around you.

Fear and Authenticity

Authenticity sounds simple in theory—just be you! But in practice, fear often disrupts the harmony between our values, identities, and actions, making authenticity far more complicated.

Whether in our personal lives or at work, we face internal fears, societal expectations, and external pressures that create dissonance between who we are and how we're expected to act. These barriers challenge our ability to lead authentically and often push us to compromise our values.

Internal Fears and Self-Judgment

Sometimes, the hardest barriers to overcome are the ones we impose on ourselves. Fear of rejection, judgment, or failure can cause us to hide parts of who we are, even from those closest to us. This fear stems from the deep human desire for acceptance and belonging. *Example: A member of the LGBTQ+ community hesitates to come out to family or colleagues, fearing rejection or exclusion. The emotional toll of hiding this core aspect of their identity can be immense, but the risk of being vulnerable feels even greater.*

Societal Norms and Expectations

Cultural norms and unspoken rules often pressure us to conform, especially in environments that value tradition over individuality. These expectations can stifle authenticity, forcing people to suppress parts of themselves that challenge established roles or stereotypes. *Example: A man avoids sharing his emotions with colleagues or friends, worried it will make him seem weak or unprofessional. This pressure to uphold traditional views of masculinity not only limits personal expression but reinforces unhealthy work-place norms.*

External Pressures in Professional Life

Workplaces often amplify these barriers, prioritizing performance over people and conformity over individuality. Leaders may feel trapped between their values and the expectations of corporate culture, forced to compromise their authenticity to meet external demands. Again, "culture fit," anyone? *Example: A manager who deeply values empathy and connection may feel forced to adopt a rigid, results-driven approach to meet company goals. This tension creates internal conflict, eroding their sense of alignment and purpose.*

This dissonance isn't just a personal struggle—it's systemic, shaped by the cultures and environments we navigate. Fear of rejection, judgment, or exclusion can feel overwhelming. In response, many of us adapt by minimizing or masking aspects of our identity to fit in or avoid perceived risks. This becomes a survival mechanism, a way to navigate environments that feel unsafe or unwelcoming. Yet while it may help us manage fear in the moment, it often comes at the cost of authenticity and connection.

Covering

One of the most common ways people cope with these barriers is by covering—a term influenced by the work of sociologist Erving Goffman.[6] Covering refers to the act of downplaying or concealing aspects of your identity to fit in or avoid negative consequences. It's not just about blending in; for many, it feels like a survival mechanism in environments where authenticity carries real risks.

This behavior shows up in many forms, including:

Code-switching. Adapting speech, behavior, or mannerisms to align with dominant cultural norms. *A person of color might change their tone or language in a predominantly white workplace to avoid standing out.*

Concealing personal struggles. Hiding emotional or physical challenges to appear more resilient. *An employee avoids discussing their mental health to prevent being perceived as less capable.*

Avoiding identity discussions. Steering clear of conversations about identity to sidestep bias or exclusion. *A queer employee chooses not to correct assumptions about their relationship status to avoid potential judgment.*

For those from marginalized groups, the stakes of uncovering are even higher. The pressure to conform isn't just about fitting in—it's about navigating systems that may not value or understand their full identities. And one last time, "culture fit," anyone?

In the short term, covering can feel like a way to protect yourself. But over time, it takes a toll. Suppressing parts of yourself creates a disconnect that can lead to exhaustion, burnout, and even a loss of identity. It's draining to constantly monitor your behavior, to wonder if being fully yourself might cost you opportunities or respect.

The costs of covering extend beyond the individual—it affects teams and organizations, too. When people don't feel safe to show up authentically, innovation suffers, collaboration falters, and trust erodes. A culture that rewards conformity over individuality misses out on the unique perspectives and creativity that diversity brings.

Ironically, the very qualities we often cover—our unique experiences, perspectives, and identities—are often what make us exceptional leaders. But breaking free from the cycle of covering requires more than just a willingness to show up authentically. It demands courage to face risks, vulnerability to embrace who we are, and self-compassion to navigate the journey.

When we challenge the systems that make covering feel necessary, we create workplaces and communities where authenticity is not just accepted but celebrated. This shift requires leaders to lead by example, fostering environments where everyone feels safe to contribute their full selves.

Kristen's Moment That Mattered: Uncovering

I had another meeting on the calendar. I always hated these, especially since they were most always contentious. The factory leaders were laser-focused on safety, build quality, production rate, and cost—so when it came to DEI, they didn't see it as a priority that was worth their most precious currency—time. I knew going in that I'd most likely be the only woman in the room again, making the case for something that most of them considered a distraction from the "real work."

This meeting felt even more unnerving because we were pushing for time to do DEI programming—one of the most undervalued business drivers in the production space. I didn't know much about the new factory leader, but I'd seen him engage with the Veteran Employee Resource Group from afar, and I made an assumption he was a veteran himself. I thought I'd try something different this time. I needed an in—a way to connect. So I wore my veteran T-shirt, with "Veteran" emblazoned across the chest. If nothing else, I figured it would give me some credibility, something to connect on.

As soon as I walked in, his team noticed the shirt. "Wait, you're a veteran?" one of them asked. I clarified that I wasn't a veteran—I was a marine. The room erupted. Marines always get that reaction—people know we're the most badass of the services, and I wore that badge with pride. The ribbing started almost immediately. The new leader had been in the army, so he was an easy target for the usual jokes. There were other veterans in the room too, but no other marines. And just like that, I was in command of the room.

We made our case for the programming. By the end of the meeting, the leader not only agreed but also asked for his entire staff to play a role. He even invited my leadership development partner back to his staff meetings for the next month, giving her precious time to discuss DEI—a rare win in these circles.

For nine years in the military, I covered a core part of my identity—my sexual orientation—believing that was the price of being seen as an effective leader. But in this moment, it wasn't covering that made the difference—it was uncovering. By choosing to reveal this part of myself, I bridged the gap between my inner game—my values and experiences—and my outer game—how I showed up in that room.

The irony wasn't lost on me. After nearly a decade of concealing who I was in order to lead, it was alignment—not hiding—that gave me the confidence to lead effectively with clarity and purpose. And while this wasn't just a win for DEI, it was a deeply personal moment of authenticity. It reinforced a simple truth: authenticity isn't just about self-expression. It's about aligning your inner game and outer game to build trust, foster connection, and inspire action.

That connection—built on mutual respect and shared identity—made all the difference. The power in that moment wasn't just in the strategy or the pitch; it was in embracing who I was and allowing my authenticity to guide the interaction. By uncovering rather than hiding, I aligned my inner and outer game, creating meaningful progress for the team while strengthening trust and rapport.

This moment demonstrated that when we lean into authenticity, we're not just staying true to ourselves; we're creating space for others to do the same. Authenticity, at its core, is about alignment—between our values, identities, and actions. When that alignment comes to life, it transforms not just how we lead but how others experience our leadership. In that shared vulnerability, real leadership begins.

Courageous Leadership and Authenticity

Courage is the foundation of authenticity. Vulnerability and self-compassion are essential elements of authenticity. Vulnerability requires us to question ourselves and dig deep for answers, confronting discomfort and uncertainty with courage. Self-compassion allows us to extend kindness to ourselves when we fall short, making room for growth and reflection rather than judgment. These elements work together to help leaders align their inner game—who they are and what they value—with their outer game—how they show up and act. By practicing vulnerability and self-compassion, courageous leaders create the foundation for authenticity, enabling them to navigate challenges with integrity and purpose.

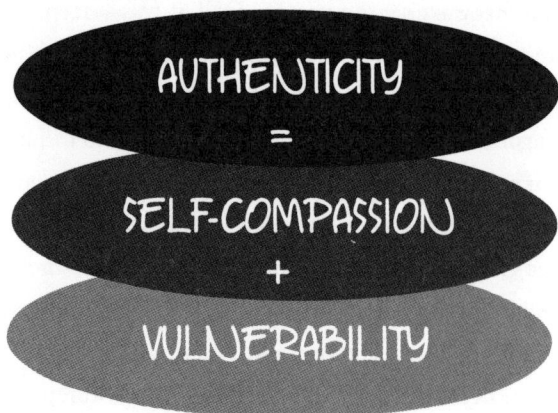

AUTHENTICITY
=
SELF-COMPASSION
+
VULNERABILITY

Vulnerability

The courage to make that kind of decision isn't just about taking bold action—it's an act of vulnerability. It requires us to face uncomfortable truths about who we are, what we value, and the fears holding us back.

> **Tab This!**
>
> Vulnerability is the ability to question
> yourself and dig deep for answers.

Vulnerability often feels risky because it pushes us into uncertainty, exposing parts of ourselves we might otherwise keep hidden. But it's also a powerful catalyst for authenticity.[7]

As leaders, vulnerability isn't a sign of weakness—it's a reflection of strength through honesty. It's about asking the tough questions: "Are we aligned with our values?" "What are we afraid of?" and "What does this moment demand of us?" These questions help us bridge the gap between our inner beliefs and outer actions, building trust and connection along the way.

When leaders embrace vulnerability, they don't just grow themselves—they set a powerful example for their teams. Modeling vulnerability creates a ripple effect, inspiring authenticity at every level of the organization. When leaders admit they don't have all the answers or acknowledge their mistakes, it fosters an environment where others feel safe to do the same. This openness builds trust, strengthens relationships, and encourages innovation by allowing diverse perspectives to emerge without fear of judgment.

Vulnerability is especially hard in the workplace, where leaders often feel the pressure to appear infallible—to have all the answers, to project confidence, and to deserve the trust of their teams. But that's the fallacy of leadership: no leader has every answer, and pretending otherwise only deepens disconnection. Leaders are human first. They have feelings and emotions. They get some things right, and they get a lot of things wrong.

And that's OK.

Vulnerability doesn't necessarily feel good. It's uncomfortable and often awkward, but it's also where real growth happens. It invites self-reflection and allows leaders to gain a deeper understanding of who they are. That self-awareness is what enables leaders to act with integrity and authenticity, even when it's risky.

Courageous leaders lean into vulnerability. They trust their ability to be open, using curiosity as a driver to explore emotions and experiences. Vulnerability requires resilience to face discomfort and navigate it thoughtfully. Courageous leaders don't shy away from these moments—they embrace them as opportunities to learn, grow, and lead with greater impact.

Self-Compassion

> **Tab This!**
>
> Self-compassion is the ability to extend kindness to yourself when you fall short of expectations.

By leaning into vulnerability, courageous leaders open themselves to self-compassion—the practice of extending grace and understanding to themselves in moments of discomfort or failure.

Together, vulnerability and self-compassion create the foundation for authenticity, enabling leaders to embrace their imperfections, build resilience, and lead with integrity and impact.

Self-compassion plays a crucial role in authenticity, especially for leaders navigating the complexities of their roles. It helps combat the negative self-talk and harsh judgment that often arise when we don't meet societal or personal standards. Practicing self-compassion takes courage—it requires leaders to acknowledge their imperfections without fear of being diminished by them. Rather than berating ourselves for falling short, self-compassion allows us to embrace imperfection, treating ourselves with the same kindness we would offer a struggling team member. This shift doesn't mean lowering our standards—it's about creating emotional balance and space for growth.[8]

Leadership is full of challenges, not least of which is the constant pressure to "get it right." Leaders often walk a fine line between the expectations placed on them and the reality of their own humanity. Self-compassion bridges that gap, allowing leaders to extend grace to themselves when they fall short while staying focused on continuous improvement.

Courage and self-compassion are deeply connected. It takes courage to admit when we've fallen short and to resist the instinct to cover our mistakes with defensiveness or self-criticism. Self-compassion, in turn, gives us the resilience to try again, to approach failure with curiosity instead of fear, and to remain aligned with our values even when we feel vulnerable.[9] This cycle of courage and self-compassion reinforces authenticity, enabling leaders to move beyond the limitations imposed by societal roles or learned behaviors.

Compassion fuels resilience. It gives leaders the strength to keep striving after setbacks, to hold space for their own growth without judgment, and to acknowledge that perfection isn't the goal. Self-compassion reminds us: "It's OK that I didn't have all the answers today." This mindset allows us to approach leadership with integrity, authenticity, and the belief that we can grow through our challenges.

Vulnerability and self-compassion are the foundation of authenticity, particularly as we navigate the complexities of our identities. Fear often arises when we feel the dissonance between who we are and how we're expected to show up. It takes courage to bring our full selves forward—both the parts the world celebrates and those it may not. But self-compassion helps us move through those fears, embracing our imperfections and honoring all facets of our identity.

Kristen's Moment That Mattered: Leaving My Identity

"Soak in all that courage," the text read as I walked away from a company that had become more than just a job—it had become my identity. My wardrobe was grayscale monochromatic. I spoke in short, punchy sentences, three bullet points max. I expected excellence. I was obsessed. To be honest, before I started working there, I hadn't even ridden in one of their products. But by the time I left, I was addicted—not just to the work, but to what it said about me. I wasn't just employed; I was part of a movement, part of something larger than myself. I owned everything that came with it—the good, the bad, and the ugly.

But after nearly six years, the dissonance became too loud to ignore. My anxiety was spiraling. My physical health was declining. The company's commitment to DEI—the very mission that drove me—was crumbling. I became a powder keg of frustration, stuck between my values and the reality around me. Yet I stayed, convincing myself I could fix it, that leaving was failure. After all, isn't leadership about pushing through, staying the course?

It wasn't until I gave myself some grace and reframed my understanding of courageous leadership that the choice became clear. Leadership isn't about endurance at the expense of your values—it's about alignment. It's about having the courage to admit when something no longer serves you or the mission. That realization came after a lot of coaching and reflection. It was a hard truth to accept, but one I couldn't ignore: I had to leave.

Making that decision was one of the hardest of my life. Walking away wasn't just about leaving a paycheck—it was about leaving an identity. Who was I without the brand, the prestige, the purpose? I feared what it said about me. I feared what others would think about me. And if I'm honest, I feared what my team would think about me. Would they see me as a quitter? A bad leader for bailing on them?

How would I find myself again? I clung to the clothes and the products, not because they defined me, but because letting them go felt like losing the last tangible pieces of that identity. I wasn't ready to separate who I was from what my time at Tesla represented to me. Truthfully, I didn't know how to let go—or how to reconcile the person I had become with the person I wanted to be.

But here's what I learned in the aftermath: courageous leadership isn't about staying in the fight just to prove you can. It's about knowing when to walk away in alignment with your values, even when the path forward is unclear—and being vulnerable enough to admit that leaving might feel like losing a part of yourself. What I came to realize was that my essence hadn't changed by leaving. My values and beliefs and the drive that brought me to the company in the first place were still there. If anything, stepping away brought me closer to my authentic self. The form—the way those values manifested—had shifted, but the core of who I was remained the same.

I didn't have to kill off that part of myself. Rather than berating myself for how deeply I had tied my identity to the company, I chose to honor the experiences that shaped me, while also making room for what came next. Self-compassion allowed me to reframe the departure—not as a failure, but as a necessary step toward growth and alignment. That job wasn't just a chapter in my life—it was a cornerstone of my growth, teaching me lessons I carry with me even now.

Leaving Tesla wasn't just an act of courage—it was an act of vulnerability and self-compassion. By choosing authenticity over fear, I allowed myself to acknowledge what I had outgrown and to trust that staying true to my values would serve me better in the long run. I gave myself permission to evolve, to let go of the need to prove myself to anyone else, and to focus on leading with clarity and purpose. And now, when I wear all black, it's not about the brand—it's about making an intentional choice to be true to myself.

Conclusion

Authenticity is the first phase of The Agency Loop and the foundation for everything that follows. It's about aligning your inner game—your values, beliefs, and identities—with your outer game—your actions and decisions. But authenticity alone isn't enough to lead courageously. To create meaningful impact, leaders must move beyond self-awareness and into intentional action. That's where the next phase of The Agency Loop, agency, comes into play. In the following chapter, we'll explore how agency transforms clarity into action, empowering leaders to make deliberate choices that align with their values and drive courageous leadership.

Make It Matter: Authenticity

Use this short exercise to help you identify where you are and the next steps to take in your journey toward courageous leadership—because it only matters if you Make It Matter.

Leading as Yourself

Authenticity is about aligning who you are with how you show up in the world. But in leadership, there are moments when being fully yourself can feel risky. External pressures, workplace expectations, or personal fears can push you to adjust or hide parts of yourself.

Reflect on a time when you felt truly authentic in your leadership—and where it may have felt harder to do so.

Take a moment to look around your workspace or think about your last few days at work. Identify three signs of values in action. These could be:

- A conversation where someone spoke openly and honestly.
- A decision that reflected a company value.
- A leader or colleague acting in a way that felt true to their beliefs.

Now Consider Yourself

- When have you felt most aligned with your values in your leadership? (Think of a recent decision or action.)

- Where do you notice tension between your values and how you feel you need to lead? (Are there situations where you hold back? Adjust your behavior? Why?)

Apply It Now—the 5 Percent More Courageous Approach

What's one action you can take this week to bring your leadership into closer alignment with your values?

AGENCY
IS POWER

CHAPTER 3

Agency

Agency is all about action. So far, we've explored how moments of dissonance arise when a leader's values clash with their environment. In the authenticity phase of The Agency Loop, leaders begin to understand that dissonance—identifying their values and identities to pinpoint where the gap exists.

The agency phase is where leaders move from awareness to action, making the decision to address the gap between their values and lived experience.

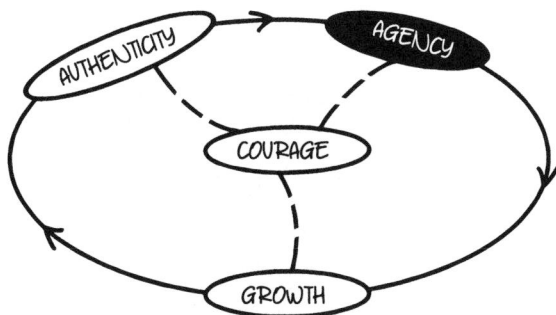

Amid the chaos of today's workplace, it can be difficult to recognize when and where you have agency. Dissonance is a call to action—but answering that call is rarely clear. It often comes with tension, and the emotions it stirs up are usually rooted in fear. But fear doesn't have to be a barrier—it can set the stage for agency.

Let's think back to Kristen's story in the previous chapter where she discussed leaving Tesla. Why do some people feel the way that Kristen felt about leaving their employers? A lot of it is based on fear. She feared losing her identity—leaving a company she deeply believed in and facing the uncertainty of what that loss might mean for her future. But that feeling could have just as easily come from the fear of loss of income and opportunities, the fear stemming from the stress of living with uncertainty, or the fear of judgment from her peers. Fear sparks powerful emotions, and like with Kristen, eventually it drives action.

But it doesn't have to be that way. Fear doesn't have to take the driver's seat. Leaders can choose actively courage over fear by exercising their agency. Courageous leadership is the ability to act with your values in the face of fear. It takes courage to recognize there is dissonance, and it also takes courage to move through it. The key really is to identify where you have agency. That is why The Agency Loop centers agency as the core mechanism for action in the face of fear.

In this chapter, we'll explore how to recognize agency and harness its power through intentionality and decisiveness. We'll start by looking at how agency first came into focus for Mike.

Mike's Moment That Mattered: The Intern

Welcoming new team members has always been one of my favorite parts of being a leader. I love harnessing the energy and fresh perspective that new team members bring, and I appreciate how those early moments of change shape their experience within an organization. Coaching interns is particularly exciting because they are sponges ready to soak up everything they can.

In the winter of 2020, I had an intern join my team. She was still finishing graduate school and eager to dive in headfirst. Tesla had huge intern cohorts each semester, and we often had several come through at a time. She was incredibly passionate about the work, logical in her organization, incredibly sharp, and quick to learn. She was well prepared too—her school and previous experience had given her as good a foundation as I could have asked for in an intern.

Yet as she stepped into the role, she had never worked at a place like Tesla before. Her experiences had come from smaller organizations, and the pace and volatility of the environment were shocking at first. She had never seen organizational turnover and uncertainty like we saw in the early days of 2020. During her time as an intern, about four months, our organization saw three new leaders come and go. She witnessed departmental reorganizations, mass terminations, project deprioritization, and widespread burnout. She saw how the work took its toll on the organization.

But with the volatility came opportunity, especially for interns. The intern program focused on giving meaningful work to interns who could help infuse new ideas into the business. During her time on my team, she helped rebuild the performance management process for the whole company—no small task, and that wasn't even her primary work. Yet even in that work, the organization surprised her. The process would be one that demanded excellence without much wiggle room for those who were not meeting expectations.

Each week, we had one-on-ones where, before we got into her project work and prioritization, we spent time connecting, getting a sense of how she was doing within the org, and generally getting to know each other a bit better. About midway through her internship, we sat down after a particularly difficult week, and she was toast. Mentally drained, physically exhausted. Of course she didn't want to let on, so she tried to hide that from me. But I noticed. I probed a bit and moved on after she remained reluctant to share with me. I'd been there before and didn't want to press it further. I knew people come to terms with wanting to talk in their own time and counted on the fact she would open up when she was ready.

So we moved on to her to-do list, starting with the project that was meant to be one of her main projects as part of the intern program. She had invested weeks on the work. This project explored the viability of building a skills-based compensation system for production workers in our factories. With thousands of employees and jobs impacted by this work, the scale and the effort needed were no small thing. She started asking questions about next steps in her work for the project, and my eyes fell. I knew I was going to have to break some jarring news to her. I shared that because of the most recent leadership transition within our organization, I was unsure if we would continue to work on the project. She was visibly frustrated now, so I gave her the space again to share. This time she took up my offer and let me have it. She was disappointed that the work could potentially stop and couldn't imagine how we ever got anything done when there was so much change, always having to look over our shoulders to see if we would be next to go.

And I had to admit, she was right. The environment was unforgiving and brutal at times. I told her as much, and to her surprise, I didn't really offer any consolation.

I'd been with the company for almost four years at that point, and she asked, "How do you stay so calm through all of this?"

I took a moment to pause and think. I thought that I was a pretty good actor because below the surface, I was not calm by any means. I wanted the project to continue just as much as her. Yet I knew that reality might be disappointing.

When I spoke, the reality of the situation came out. "I guess I just assume that I'm already dead here, so why not do the best I can while I have the time?"

Initially, she was mortified that I had been so forthcoming with her. She sat back to process, and I continued. "You only have the ability to control what you do here, how you act and how you behave. You can't control anyone else, and certainly not the organization. I choose to do the things that I believe are right for the organization and align with my values, and if that means that I am going to be fired because of it, then so be it. I can live with myself when I go to bed at night." Her posture softened, and I could see that the gravity of what I shared was sinking in.

She asked how I had come to those terms, and I told her about a book that had dramatically shaped my worldview—*Man's Search for Meaning*, by Viktor Frankl.[1] I shared my experience reading it, then ordered her a copy and encouraged her to give it a read. After that, we moved on with the meeting.

Viktor Frankl is a renowned psychologist and survivor of the atrocities of World War II. I had read *Man's Search for Meaning* the previous year in search of a better understanding of how to retain my humanity while working in a toxic environment. I was desperately looking for answers, as I saw good leaders and colleagues continuously leave the company. What I found in the book was transformational because it gave me a sense of perspective that I could never have imagined.

In the book Frankl describes how he found meaning from his experiences in WWII. Frankl's core message is the realization through his experiences that while he was unable to control almost anything in his life during that time under Nazi occupation, he remained free in his own mind to choose how he would respond to those external circumstances. He goes on to elaborate that this power to choose how you respond, given any set of circumstances, gives you the opportunity to define meaning in your life and act based on that new understanding.

While it was an abrupt introduction to Frankl's core concept, the introduction for my intern helped her to better understand where she had power in that situation where she felt otherwise powerless. Eventually her internship came to an end with Tesla, but she hadn't been scared away. Rather, we extended her the opportunity to stay on for another term, where she eventually joined the organization full time.

What I didn't know at the time was that Frankl's work would be a cornerstone for my worldview. My experience was nowhere near as extreme as his, but it set in motion a mindset shift about who I could be and how I could act. The exploration of those themes led to the creation of this book, and ultimately how we view Agency.

Agency Is Power

Power and control are often closely linked because control is how power is maintained. But leadership isn't about holding on—it's about knowing when to let go. Power might mean that a leader can make decisions without facing the consequences, regardless of the outcome. It often comes with protections (e.g., job roles and titles, financial stability, lack of organizational accountability) that shield individuals from repercussions. Those protections create a buffer against the very conditions that generate dissonance and emotions like fear. But for the vast majority of people who live in the real world, our actions have consequences, and we know it.

Fear is amplified by a person's perception of their locus of control—how much power they believe they have to influence a situation and where that power comes from. In the story, the intern had virtually no control whatsoever on whether or not the project moved forward. She couldn't make the decision to continue on with the project, a cornerstone of her experience with the company and a key consideration in the offer of full-time employment. It is in moments like this where we often see a sense of powerlessness, particularly for emerging leaders who are facing situations like this for the first time and for leaders who are in the middle layers of management who often feel pressure coming from all directions.

We are willing to bet that everyone reading this book has felt powerless at some point. We have. We felt powerless when we received the mandate to return to the office. We felt powerless when we faced a third round of layoffs within a year. We felt powerless when we were told to figure out how to train over thirty thousand leaders on respect in the workplace on a tight timeline and a shoestring budget.

In many cases, we didn't recognize until later that our sense of powerlessness wasn't coming from within—it was a product of the situation we were in. It was easy to focus on where we lacked power, reinforcing a cycle of learned helplessness—the belief that our actions wouldn't make a difference. But when we flipped the narrative and shifted our focus toward where we did have power, we began to see the places where we had agency.

This is where the core of Frankl's work gives power to agency. Frankl found freedom in the worst possible conditions because he sought out where he still had some control rather than be bound by what he couldn't do. The power of agency is in the recognition that you always have agency. Everyone. Every leader. We use this as a starting point for discussing agency because the fear of the consequences often makes leaders feel powerless in situations where the environment and the experience feel out of their control. So leaders have to look for it and explore what control they do have.

If you take nothing else away from this chapter, remember: you have agency.

> **Tab This!**
>
> ### You have agency.

We couldn't change the mandate to return to the office, but we could give people the opportunity to opt out with the support they needed to find roles that worked for them. We couldn't stop layoffs, but we could commit to creating space for human emotion, processing change, and searching for the path forward. We didn't have the power to mandate broader changes in addition to the training for every leader to actually create a respectful workplace, but we could ensure that our message in the training was clear, meaningful, and genuine so that every leader who attended the training understood what was expected of them and how they needed to behave as a human. And if you remember, we shared that the intern came back for another internship term and received a full-time offer. The project never picked back up. Her decision to move forward, continue to learn, and focus her effort in the places she could make an impact made our choice to hire her easy.

We found power where we could by orienting our intentions to find the best possible outcomes, given the set of circumstances we faced. The mindset shift from external locus of power to an internal locus of power gave clarity where our intentions could be brought to life. Too often, leaders wait until they feel safe to take action, some external locus of power like a job title or permission from someone they see as being an authority. Courageous leaders seek outcomes that align with their values, which address the dissonance they experience, and then act to bring those outcomes to life.

Agency Defined

If you have felt like agency, in the way it has been used in this book, is nebulous, you are not alone. It took us a while to sort out what we meant when we use the word *agency*. It isn't a term that many people use frequently. The most common usage of the word is to describe a firm that is representative of a body of work or talented individuals. Think advertising, marketing, creative, public relations, or other representative agencies. That's what usually pops into folks' minds when we start to talk to them about agency. It used to bother us when we would get called "the Agency" or "an Agency," or have clients reach out, thinking that we were there to represent them. Now it's our internal way of telling to see if someone is really paying attention to our work. Or if they are just being polite. The point is, it isn't often that we meet someone who truly understands and internalizes the concept of agency in the way we mean it. So we want to be clear in what we are talking about here.

Agency is the ability to make intentional decisions based on your values. We want every leader to be able to make decisions that authentically reflect who they are and how they choose to show up as a leader. Agency represents the power you have to take action in every circumstance.

> **Tab This!**
>
> Agency is the ability to make intentional decisions based on your values.

OK, so you now know how to define it, but *how* do you exercise agency? There are three things you need to consider as a leader.

1. Recognize where you have agency. Agency is often masked in terms of control or power, but in an organization, every leader has agency. It is up to the leader to discover the power of their agency.
2. Determine the intentional outcomes. You need to know how the outcomes you want to achieve deliberately align with your values.
3. Decide on your course of action and act. Agency is about action, running the internal calculus on what you can do to achieve your intentional outcomes and then taking action.

Courageous Leadership and Agency

We introduced the power of agency earlier because many leaders don't initially recognize when and where they have it. Agency is one of the most integral components of courageous leadership because it empowers leaders to make decisions and take action in alignment with their values, even in the face of uncertainty. It's not enough to simply recognize your values—courageous leaders must act on them.

The real test of agency isn't just understanding the elements of intentionality and decisiveness; it's knowing how to bring them together when it matters most. Intentionality gives leaders the clarity to act purposefully, ensuring their decisions reflect core beliefs. Decisiveness, on the other hand, equips them to confidently choose a course of action, even in the face of risks or unknowns. Together, these elements form a mental calculus—one that balances the purpose of the outcome you're aiming for with the key variables you must consider.

This practice of agency allows leaders to move beyond passive awareness and create meaningful, values-driven actions that foster trust, drive progress, and shape organizational culture. Throughout the chapter, we'll explore how these elements relate to agency and how they work together to drive courageous leadership. To get started, let's look at an example of how intent and impact can sometimes be misaligned in a phrase almost everyone has heard before.

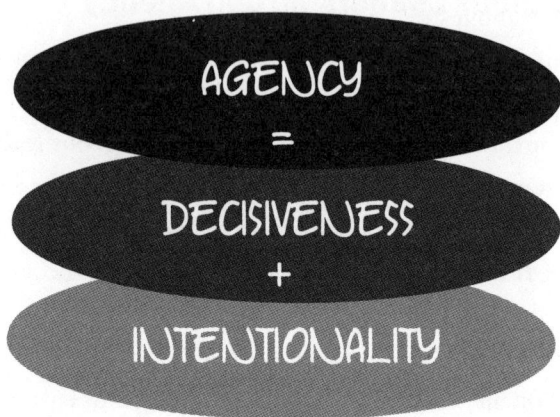

AGENCY
=
DECISIVENESS
+
INTENTIONALITY

Intentionality: Aiming Your Agency

"But I didn't mean to hurt him . . . "

We are both parents of pairs of rough-and-tumble little boys. As parents of young boys, though, we would need far more fingers and toes than we have collectively to count the number of times we have heard them say, "But I didn't mean to hurt him" after the tears have started flowing.

"I didn't mean to hurt him" is a perfect example of when someone realizes their mistake after the fact but didn't think beforehand about the potential impact of their actions.

What often starts off as playing, joking, teasing, wrestling, or any other seemingly innocent action ends up causing hurt, tears, pain, or fear. Those little boys are children, though, who don't yet fully understand that actions have impacts, outcomes, and consequences. And we wouldn't expect them to be experts at it. Our oldest boys are just now starting to understand outcomes as they progress through elementary school. The equation they have in their heads about situations is often pretty simple. Something like:

"I think that potty jokes are funny, so when I call my brother a potty name, it will be funny too."

Obviously that is a really basic example, but shows that even at a very young age, we are starting to think through the decisions we make. We should expect that as they transition from children to adults, the math gets a little more sophisticated.

Leaders face a more complex equation. We often refer to this as "doing the calculus"—evaluating the various factors that could impact a decision and determining the best course of action based on those considerations. For a leader, that could look like navigating the right conditions to give a team member feedback, to advocate for a team member to be promoted, or even when to pick up the phone and call someone instead of sending another email.

> **Tab This!**
>
> Intentionality is the ability to act in a deliberate
> way with a certain outcome in mind.

We found that the "calculus" is different for everyone, so there's no one-size-fits-all formula. Intentionality is the driving force behind that equation. We define intentionality as acting in a deliberate way with a certain outcome in mind. And really that means two things. Leaders have to decide who they want to be in their actions (think authenticity) and what the outcome of a decision means in relation to their values (think purpose). This is how inner game and outer game show up in agency. The inner game involves the mindset, values, and beliefs that guide who you are in the moment of action—how you show up as a leader. The outer game is the manifestation of those values in the actions you take and the impact you create. To break this down further, let's look at agency in terms of authenticity in action.

Agency as Authenticity in Action

Intentionality means two things as part of agency. The first is the intention a leader has in how they represent themselves in their actions. We want leaders to show up authentically. Back in chapter 2, we explored what it means to be authentic as a leader. We explored how our values act as our anchor for how we navigate the world and that our identities are how we and others see ourselves in the world. That means that the work they have done to figure out who they will show up as a leader, their values, beliefs, and identities comes through in the way they act. Agency is a moment of choice, and in that moment, we want leaders to bring forth that authenticity in the choices they make.

Intention begins with understanding yourself and your perspective. That's why our definition of agency is rooted in values. All the work a leader does to understand their values and identities provides the foundation for their decisions in moments of action. We see this as the starting point of agency because it grounds a leader's choices in what matters most to them. Intention is the decision a leader makes about how they want to show up and what actions they will take to achieve a specific outcome.

For example, we have navigated organizational change quite a bit in our experience. In organizational change, transparency in communication builds trust.[2] Because of that, when we received notice of an organizational change, we often wanted to get that information to our team as soon as possible. We knew we could take a number of different actions, like send an email with the information, call a team meeting in the moment, tell each member individually, or wait until the next team meeting or company all-hands. All of these could be potential ways we could have relayed that information to our team.

Here is where the calculus came into play. We had to determine which method best builds trust through transparency in this situation. Because we intended to build trust, we had to go through the possibilities of what we could do and determine what our intention was for the outcome. We asked ourselves, Do we need to be the first to build trust? Or do we need to make sure that we tell everyone at the same time? Would the team rather hear it from us or from our leaders? This is where the action we picked in this situation needed to align with our desired outcome.

Where the exploration of the intention in a decision gets tricky is in the decision's impact. Leaders not only have to determine what they intend the impact or outcome to be of the action, but they also need to review how their team may perceive the outcome of the action. If the perception of the team is different from what the leader intended for the outcome, the gap between those two could impact the team's trust in the leader, making the action one that actually breaks down trust rather than building it up. This illustrates not only the complexity leaders face in making decisions but also underscores how one organization or team is not the same as the other.

Agency as Purpose in Action

The second component of intentionality within agency is the desired outcome a leader has based on the decisions they make. What makes this powerful is not just in how a leader uses their authenticity in the choice or decision they make, but also how they can use it to engineer a desired outcome. Leaders shouldn't aim to control outcomes necessarily—that can feel like manipulation and walk a fine line between using fear to lead rather than courage. Rather, leaders should seek to influence outcomes through planning and determining risk.

Let's revisit the example of our desire for transparency during organizational change. The decision calculus starts to take shape as we weigh our options for transparently communicating with the team. When facing an impending change, we considered various methods of sharing the news. Based on our relationship with the team and the organization's culture, we often found that options like waiting for the all-hands meeting or sending an email wouldn't produce the desired outcome. Both could deliver the message, but our experience showed that their impersonal nature wouldn't build trust in the same way that more direct communication would.

To clarify, we based this example on our experience, but other leaders may have more authentic practices for delivering this message to their teams. Each leader who knows their team and understands team norms and communication styles is better equipped to determine the right course of action for their situation. That's why there is no one-size-fits-all approach. We knew our teams wanted to hear directly from us, and we recognized our responsibility to model how to deliver difficult information. In turn, our teams understood their responsibility to share that information with their organizations in a way that was authentic to them.

Leaders who practice intentionality recognize that when they deliberately align their decisions with a specific goal, they can choose actions most likely to drive the desired results. This approach helps them cultivate influence—the ability to shape outcomes without relying on direct authority or pressure. Effective influence extends beyond individual teams, shaping direction and momentum across an entire organization.

Influence versus Manipulation

Just like we mentioned the juxtaposition of intention and control, we also need to think carefully about how courageous leaders should balance influence with manipulation. For our purposes, we would consider influence as achieving a desired effect or outcome, but that also aligns with organizational goals, the values of individual leaders and an organization, and that has a net positive effect.

Manipulation on the other hand, in this context, we consider as the attempt to control or play upon by unfair, or insidious means, especially to one's own advantage.[3] This runs counter to the assumption of positive intention that we hold as foundational for courageous leadership. Manipulation is a tool of a fear-based leader, seeking to control while minimizing the voices. The tools of a courageous leader exercising agency, intention, and influence are powerful mechanisms to drive organizational change and performance.

Decisiveness: Running the Calculus

Intentionality alone doesn't fully define agency. Our definition of agency is the ability to make decisions aligned with your values.

While intentionality ensures your actions reflect your values and purpose, decisiveness plays a critical role in the calculus. It involves evaluating all the variables that influence your decision, helping you choose the best course of action with confidence.

Decisiveness is making clear, confident decisions that align with your values and priorities. Leaders who are decisive make values-aligned decisions with clarity and conviction in Moments That Matter, embracing both the responsibility and consequences of those actions. Courage is required to look at the risks and interpret external factors that may impact how much a leader can control in the decision, while maintaining alignment to purpose in the process. That's a lot. We know. It felt like a lot coming up with the definition, so we'll take some time to unpack it, and hopefully set off some light bulbs along the way. To help set the stage, we'll share another story to use as our example.

Mike's Moment That Mattered: The Role of a Lifetime

In 2019, I was firmly embedded in the culture at Tesla. I had started my journey at the company through the hotly contested acquisition of SolarCity finalized in 2017. I had pivoted from what was a laidback, solar-for-all vibe at SolarCity to drinking the Tesla

Kool-Aid and the survival-at-all-costs mentality prevalent across the company. When I made that transition, it felt like a necessity to be all in—partially because the company had gone through three massive layoffs over the course of eighteen months but partially in part, too, because I had seen so many of my former colleagues at SolarCity be the casualties of those layoffs. I felt like I owed it to the people whom I had to say goodbye to over the course of that time. Many were hardworking and talented folks, and I felt like I had to do everything that I could with the opportunities and time given to me to honor them. I felt like I had something to prove.

I wasn't the only one who felt like this. At some point my close group of colleagues and friends all came to realize that it was a place where everyone felt like they had to play the game to win. Like there was always some advantages to be gained, some angle to take to get ahead. To be frank, I hated it. I felt like most days at work, I was leaving part of my soul behind because of the toll the constant strategizing, maneuvering, dealmaking, and posturing to win at all costs took on my spirit.

I was lucky to have a tight-knit group of colleagues with whom I could share frustrations, strategies, and stories. We were all emerging leaders and HR program managers, still learning how to navigate our fast-changing environment.

In the fall of 2019, one of those colleagues announced she was leaving the company to join a former manager who had recently resigned. I was happy for her—though admittedly a bit envious of her chance to step off the roller coaster. Her departure left open a high-visibility role overseeing the company's performance management system. I knew that if I landed it, it could be a major step forward in my career.

I saw my window of opportunity, and the cultural conditioning that I had experienced to that moment kicked in. My colleague that was leaving told our small group of us her intention to leave days before she shared with our leadership team at the time. Immediately, I started thinking of how I could make her departure an opportunity for me. If I got out ahead of the announcement by telling my leader, I might be able to secure the role. I thought to myself that I could spin my actions in telling my boss that it would help the leadership team save face in the wake of another departure by making it look like they had a transition plan for such an impactful role in the company.

But in the same moment, I felt the dissonance. I knew that the group of leaders she trusted with the news also trusted me. That trust represented the kind of colleague, leader, and friend that I wanted to be. There was a gap between my desire to maintain trust with that group and my desire to step into the role after my boss left. I didn't want to leave it to chance, and the fear of losing the opportunity weighed heavily on me. For two days I wavered back and forth between the decision to reach out to the hiring manager before my boss's official announcement to the leadership team or keep my mouth shut and pray. I knew what my values told me was the right thing to do, but I couldn't shake the fear of the potential loss.

At the end of that second day, I called another colleague whom I trusted who was outside the team. I told them of the battle going on in my mind. We talked briefly on the impact that my decision to reach out early could have on my credibility, how those closest to me would view me afterward, and the loss of trust that my actions would cause. It was a defining moment and decision of who I would show up as at work.

I had to decide who I was going to be and how I was going to show up. Despite my anxiety, I chose to wait. I waited until the announcement of the departure was made to share my desire and intention to seek the role. And for the thirty-six hours or so between when I made the decision to wait and the announcement, I was a mess internally, running all the possibilities where the role would not end up coming to me. I knew it could be a role of a lifetime, but I also knew that I wouldn't really be me if I made the decision to go against my values. I held firm in that decision, and it paid off. Within a day of my colleague making the public announcement that she was leaving, I was talking with her former manager about my qualifications and vision for the role, and within two weeks, I had the job. I held true to my values while achieving the result I wanted. I've made plenty of other decisions in my career that didn't turn out well, but this one did.

Action versus Inaction

Agency is a call to action—action based on the values that you worked so hard to understand and used to build your authentic self around. It is ultimately the action you take that will define success in those moments. When we break it down, though, the action you take is more complex than just doing it. We have run the decision calculus to get a sense of all the different considerations, like timing, risks, the desired outcomes, consequences, and even the advantages you might have that feed into the moment of action.

But sometimes the greatest battle a leader can wage is whether or not to do anything at all. In the story we just shared, inaction (well, delayed action—more on that in a moment) triumphed over the desire to take advantage of the situation. In terms of agency, though, any leader has to take stock of the situation at hand to determine whether action is indeed needed at all or if inaction would serve the purpose better. That decision, to take action or not, is always within a leader's power.

Yet far too often, when met with a critical decision or a challenge to overcome, leaders spring into action, motivating their team to dive in headfirst and get to work. Action is perceived as success because it gives leaders something tangible to tie outcomes back to. And in many cases, inaction is perceived as failure, as leaders are characterized as lazy, fearful, or incompetent. Leaders are tasked with the success of their teams, and the fear of being called any of those labels is powerful enough to compel them to take action, even if their internal tensions are telling them not to. It takes courage to listen to those feelings and to align what you do, even if it means you do nothing.

Timing

Now you might be saying, "Wait just a minute. I am faced with decisions every day that I have to make in the moment."

That's absolutely true. But we would challenge your assumption that a decision has to be made so quickly. In Mike's story, timing was the key to turning an opportunistic trust-destroying action, albeit with good intentions, into a trust-building moment. Leaders have to be willing to get curious about the moments they face.

This is where as you look at the variables of the situation, you should be exploring what are the right questions to ask about the timing of your decisions and actions. Are you making an assumption that a decision needs to be made right away? Are you making assumptions about the outcomes because of the timing?

Because every organization and situation is different, we can't tell you the right timing to act. You will ultimately know your organizations and its norms for timing better than we can. Courage here, though, is to be willing to sit with the discomfort of the dissonance long enough to get curious about the timing.

Acting at the right moment can define the difference between success and failure. Decisiveness in agency isn't about moving fast. What a courageous leader does is get curious about the right timing for a decision and then act with confidence in the decision.

Risk

No conversation around decision-making would be complete without a healthy discussion on risk. As we researched the book, we found a number of actual risk calculators, formulas, and variables that could be considered when making decisions. It doesn't have to be that complicated, though, and most of the time, you are making the risk calculation while another part of your brain is yelling at you that you are running out of time.

Risk represents a leader's exploration of uncertainty and the potential outcomes associated with the decision. Many times it involves negative outcomes. In Mike's story it came down to something very simple. Would the outcome of circumventing his colleague's plan and sharing her intention to leave outweigh the potential damage to his reputation and relationships in the workplace? Would that be authentic to the leader he wanted to be? It is not going to be simple in all cases, and each individual leader is going to have to determine their boundaries.

When a leader is able to determine their boundaries, it liberates them to make decisions that either reinforce or protect their values and identities. In the story context, it was inaction that protected Mike's values and identities. Yet in other cases, action helps push those boundaries. This is where the exploration of uncertainty can lead to positive outcomes.

Remember the 5 percent more courageous approach? We encourage leaders to experiment by testing boundaries in Moments That Matter. Courageous leaders trust themselves and stay curious, allowing these experiments to reveal new insights. Understanding the risks in a decision enables leaders to align their intentions and take action with conviction.

Pragmatic Outcomes versus Purposeful Outcomes

We started the discussion of outcomes when we looked at purpose in intentionality, aligning the outcomes of actions with a specific purpose that represents who you are authentically. In other words, the outcome of your action represents your values and identities on purpose. Yet a purposeful outcome is not always a pragmatic outcome. Pragmatic outcomes often center around achieving specific, often immediate outcomes through efficient and expedient means. Again, thinking about the example in Mike's moment, it may have been pragmatic for his career to share the departure news right away in service of getting the new job. And while that could have turned into a short-term gain for him, it may have had ripple effects in the consequences that came from his action.

To be clear, the pragmatic approach is not always a different option than the purposeful approach; it also may yield the same desired outcome (e.g., getting the role of a lifetime). Yet courage is needed in the decision to avoid the temptation of a pragmatic outcome when getting curious about what each would mean for you as a leader. Introspection is hard, particularly when running this calculus in real time. Courageous leaders trust that the process of introspection and curiosity fuels meaningful action.

Consequences

Here is the deal, though. While it is helpful to understand the timing, risk and outcomes, courageous leaders have to be willing to own the impact of their outcomes, better known as the consequences of their actions, much like they will be required to navigate the impact of their decisions. Consequences represent the good and the bad, the intended and the unintended, from the decisions that are made. Consequences could be something immediate, or something that is long term. In Mike's case, had he chosen to go against his instinct and let the cat out of the bag, it is likely that he would have experienced the long-term consequence of loss of trust within the organization.

Courageous leaders embrace the responsibility for owning consequences through agency. If agency is a reflection of the leader, a values-based decision, then the leader must take responsibility for that action. That isn't to say external circumstances will never play a role, but the buck stops with a courageous leader. Courageous leaders don't push blame on others or run from responsibility. Rather, they lean into the accountability of their decisions, offering transparency in their reasoning and reflection in their wake. Most importantly, courageous leaders admit their mistakes. The fallout, the failure, the success, and the growth that all come from these decisions are the leader's to weather, and in that responsibility, a courageous leader builds resilience and models growth.

Privilege

Decision calculus isn't complete without looking at the role privilege plays in a leader's ability to take action. This is a hot button, and we get that, so before we jump into the role it plays for leaders, let's stop and get curious about what it means.

Privilege is often described as unearned advantages, rights, or benefits that an individual or group possesses because of a status, role, or title they may have within a system (like where you work). Those benefits are seen as unearned because they often come with the role, status, or title regardless of the efforts of an individual or in our case, leader, that assumes that role, status, or title. It is there because of the system, not because of the individual.[4]

This becomes a hot-button issue because when we focus on individual leaders, a dissonance arises between their experience of earning a role, status, or title and the unearned benefits that come with it. In other words, a leader may have worked hard their whole life to get to a job, and might feel that because of their hard work, they deserve all of the advantages that come with that role. But here is the thing: those advantages would have existed regardless of their hard work. They are baked into the system.

This doesn't invalidate a leader's lived experience. It is possible that a leader may have worked hard to achieve their role and status, but it is also possible that the role and status have structural advantages for that leader and their team. It takes courage for leaders to set aside feelings, especially defensiveness, to truly acknowledge the advantages their role gives them. Leaders inherently have more privilege than those who are not in leadership roles. Yet even within leadership, there are varying degrees of privilege based on other factors (e.g., gender, age, ethnicity, disability, socioeconomic status, work assignments). No two experiences within leadership are the same. To be a courageous leader, you have to get curious about your own privileges, where the privilege comes from, and take it into account during your calculation.

Our Moment That Mattered: When Privilege Shapes Agency

We were on the cusp of launching The Agency Initiative and wanted to make sure we weren't delusional in our focus on courage and agency. The first time we rolled out The Agency Loop, in a very loose concept, was with a team of former colleagues and trusted advisers. They knew the dissonance a place like Tesla could cause all too well: haphazard RIFs, botched return-to-the-office policies, executives disappearing in the middle of the night, and loyalists elevated without a single leadership qualification. They had fought side by side in the toxic trenches with us through all of it. For a variety of reasons, they had all made very personal choices about their careers vis-à-vis Tesla. Some had moved on. Others were still fighting the good fight on the inside. All were invested in helping us help leaders step into their courage and live aligned with their values.

In the last feedback session, one of the leaders came in hot: "So you are going to tell a production associate working a twelve-hour shift on the production line, who also happens to be a single mom, to go out and exercise her agency every time she feels like this place is out of alignment with her values? You're going to get people fired!" she exclaimed.

No, that wasn't what we were planning to do, but she had a point.

Yes, even the production associates on the line had agency. They made choices all day, every day. But for many of them, their calculus was different. It had to be.

Not everyone has the luxury of telling their employer to pound sand when they cross a line. The truth is, people have all kinds of reasons for them to stay. They stay because the financial burden of leaving—a potential pay cut, loss of retirement contributions, or the uncertainty of finding a comparable role—feels too risky to bear. They stay because the health insurance is too good to give up. They stay because they believe in the mission. They stay because their job is tied to their identity and community. They stay because their employment is tied to a work visa. They stay because they hold out hope that things will improve. While some have the privilege of walking away, many don't have that luxury—they make deeply personal calculations to navigate the tension between agency and survival.

That luxury is privilege, and it comes in all different forms from different sources.

What our colleague pointed out was that we had to be explicit about addressing the role privilege plays in the loop, specifically in a leader's ability to exercise their agency.

So let us be explicit. You have agency. And with great power comes great responsibility—to understand the privilege you hold and how it shapes the choices available to you. Privilege isn't inherently good or bad, but ignoring it can lead to blind spots that hinder your ability to act courageously and align with your values and possibly get you fired.

Navigating Privilege

Privilege creates advantages (e.g., access to resources and information, greater implicit authority, and organizational safety). Leaders who experience privilege often feel more willing to fail because they often have a bigger safety net and organizational support to recover. And because of that, privilege tips the scales on a leader's willingness and confidence to take risks and make bolder decisions. The burden of responsibility for consequences shifts in instances of decision-making from privilege. Their status protects them from the same scrutiny and accountability that others might face.

We felt compelled to add this to the decision calculus because we know that privilege is not the same for every leader. We know there may be a first-time supervisor reading this book, or a single parent, or someone who covers their true identity at work out of fear. All leaders are going to be faced with decisions that create tension between the situation and their values and identities. But not every leader is in a position to be able to suffer the consequences of their decisions. What we mean here is that you might know what you would do, how you would act, but still wouldn't act on it because you didn't have the title, the organizational position, favorable demographics, or even in more basic terms, the financial means or personal safety to be able to weather the outcomes of your decisions. It's a privilege to not have to think about those things. We often had to ask ourselves, Would this decision get me fired or ostracized? When it did, we had to make a different choice—one of self-preservation. So might you when the moment comes. Certain circumstances require us to choose self-preservation. And that is OK.

We are going to say it again for the folks in the back. Choosing self-preservation when you have to is OK.

The process of this loop, of figuring out who you are as a leader, taking action based on that, and learning from it is not about wearing everything on your sleeves. It's not about being a martyr either. It is about your journey to making decisions that are representative of your values, understanding the risks, and living to fight another day, both in how you live with the choices that you make, and how those choices keep you in the game longer. Because the world needs more courageous leaders. Leaders who are willing to accept the burden of their choices made from their values. The world needs leaders who understand the power of their agency.

Mike's Moment That Mattered: Chief of Staff

The fall of 2021 felt like a turning point for many people. The pandemic seemed to be coming under control, and at work, there seemed to be a settling into what life might look like post pandemic. I'd been leading my team for well over a year at that point, and the leaders on my team were dialed in. Projects were humming along; programs continued to expand, building stability and consistency into the employee experience. The progress and stability felt good after navigating years of change.

Outside of my team, though, I felt there was still a ton of work to be done, both within HR and the company. Because my team was performing at such a high level, it freed up some of my time to begin to look across the organization to continue to deepen what we called the "connective tissue," things like relationships and organizational efficiencies, all in the service of continuing to improve the employee experience. But like you might expect, you can only do so much when the role you are in is limited to a certain scope of work.

Yet serendipity finds a way to rear its head. During that same time period, the leader of HR began realizing that for the organization to grow, it would require someone to focus specifically on cross-functional projects. These were the type of complex projects that required deep understanding of how the HR organization worked together, and the type of never-say-never mentality that everyone was so accustomed to within the company. I was feeling really comfortable with the success of my team, as we had implemented numerous projects across the organization that fit that mold.

More importantly, this leader was looking for someone to act as her boots on the ground in getting the work done. The person in the role would play a key part in driving HR strategy for the company and would have access to the highest-level decision-makers across the organization. (I hope you are getting the sense that I was excited about the opportunity, because I was.)

This was a big step, and the timing felt right. It felt right for my team and for my leaders. It felt right for the organization to take the next step in its growth, as Tesla had well over one hundred thousand employees, and HR needed to keep pace. And it felt right for me personally. I had just settled into a new home with my family in Austin, Texas, and we were ready to start building our lives around our new community.

When the requirements for the role were finally posted, I wanted to rush into submitting myself for consideration, but I hesitated. My calculus was kicking in. The role opened at a more junior level than I had expected. Role leveling and hierarchy meant something within the organization, and I knew that something as simple as a junior title could impact my ability to influence within the organization and with our cross-functional stakeholders. This was a risk.

I sought counsel. Kristen was my leader at the time. We circled the wagons and ran through what it could mean for me to apply for the role as posted. We ran through all the pros and cons, and what I could do to make it work. We ran the calculus together. Ultimately, I decided the potential impact the role could have within the organization was too great, and I thought I could help.

So I submitted my name for consideration.

When it came time to interview with the hiring manager, our HR executive, I got curious about the leveling of the role. I also explained that I saw the opportunity in the role in spite of the risk. We discussed how the role represented the opportunity to help the HR organization coalesce around her leadership and drive her strategic initiatives. Her vision was for the person who stepped into the role to serve as her chief of staff in everything but the title. We didn't have "chief of staff" titles in the company, but people with responsibilities existed covertly in some parts of the business under comparable titles. I left that conversation feeling energized, knowing that the scope of the role was more expansive than the description had led on and could have a meaningful impact on the HR organization's effectiveness across the company. I was ready to dive in.

I got the job, and dive in, I did. Shortly after we announced I would be stepping into the role, I got my first major assignment. I was tasked with building and leading a high-priority program to train every leader in the company. By every leader, that meant more than thirty thousand leaders. By training, that meant offering an instructor-facilitated experience. Me. I was the instructor. Yet I was optimistic. I decided to take this role. This was the work I had signed up for, and I was ready to take on the task.

I took a risk, and my decision paid off. Until it didn't . . .

Conclusion

Agency is the second phase of The Agency Loop, where clarity turns into action. It's about making intentional decisions based on your values, even when the path ahead is uncertain. But understanding agency is just the beginning—it's something you practice. The courage to act is a key part of agency; without courage, even the clearest decisions can remain unmade. When you actively practice agency, you move from awareness to action, building trust in your ability to lead with courage.

With agency in hand, you're ready for the next phase: growth. This phase challenges you to transform past tensions into actionable insights, using those lessons to shape future decisions and evolve into your next version of yourself. It's where you make meaning from your experiences, refine your identity, and prepare for what's next. In the following chapter, we'll explore how practicing agency allows leaders to turn their experiences into growth and use the power of intentional action to plan for the future.

Make It Matter: Agency

Use this exercise to help you identify where you are and the next steps to take in your journey toward courageous leadership—because it only matters if you Make It Matter.

How Do You Make Leadership Decisions?

Every leader has a unique way of deciding when to act. Some focus on timing, others on relationships, and others on risk. Instead of following a one-size-fits-all formula, leaders develop their own way of thinking through decisions.

What Do You Consider?

Think about a recent leadership decision—big or small. Maybe you gave feedback, advocated for someone, or decided when to speak up.

What were the biggest things on your mind when making that choice?

- Your values—What felt right?
- The situation—What was happening around you?
- The risks—What could go wrong? What could go right?
- Your role—How did your position affect the choice?
- The consequences—What did you have to gain? What did you have to lose?
- Other considerations—What else shaped your decision?

What's Your Approach?

Look at what shaped your decision. What is your decision calculus? How do you typically decide when to act?

For example:

- "I focus on what feels right first, then think about timing before I move forward."
- "I weigh how my decision will affect people, then consider risks and benefits before acting."
- "If something aligns with my values and helps my team, I take action even if it feels risky."

Apply It Now—the 5 Percent More Courageous Approach

Think about a decision you need to make soon. How can you use your decision calculus to decide what to do?

FIND
OPPORTUNITY

CHAPTER 4

Growth

Growth brings forth the essence of courageous leadership—an opportunity to evolve, adapt, and lead with intention. Yet despite its importance, growth is often misunderstood. Too often, we assume it happens naturally, like the passing of time, rather than something we cultivate.

Through this book, we have argued that The Agency Loop is the key to unlocking growth. But even we found ourselves staring into the void when trying to define how growth truly works. We explored authenticity as the phase where your values and identities meet reality, and agency as the phase where action aligns intention. But when it came to articulating growth, we found ourselves staring at a blank page, struggling to put words to something we had long taken for granted.

And that is the problem. It is easy to take growth for granted because time moves forward, whether we engage with the outcomes of our decisions or not. We've heard leaders say they don't know where to begin, that the conditions for growth never seem right, or that they are simply too busy. In workplaces where production is king, there is always another deadline, another initiative, another release. Growth seems like a luxury.

But the truth is, growth isn't something that happens in the margins—it happens in the Moments That Matter. While estimates vary, research suggests that people make tens of thousands of decisions daily, with the majority occurring subconsciously and automatically as part of habitual cognitive processing.[1] However, among these countless choices are defining moments—opportunities where we can choose to grow or remain the same. The challenge lies in recognizing these moments and understanding their significance.

Even when we do take time to reflect—through retrospectives or postmortems—the process often feels incomplete. These meetings help us improve projects or how work gets done, but rarely create space for individual growth. And let's be honest, *postmortem* is a telling term. How often do we treat growth like an autopsy, only examining it after the fact?

As we examined the barriers to growth, one truth became inescapable: growth is not easy. It forces us to relive difficult moments, critique ourselves honestly and embrace the discomfort in that critique. That is why growth isn't passive—it demands courage. The courage to face tension. The courage to acknowledge where we fell short. The courage to change.

The growth phase of The Agency Loop challenges leaders to harness that courage, transforming past experiences into actionable insights, shaping future decisions and future versions of themselves. It is in this phase that leaders make meaning from their experiences, refine their identities, and plan for what lies ahead. To do this, we had to rethink how we approached reconciling with moments of tension. We needed to understand how the decision calculus generated both outcomes and consequences.

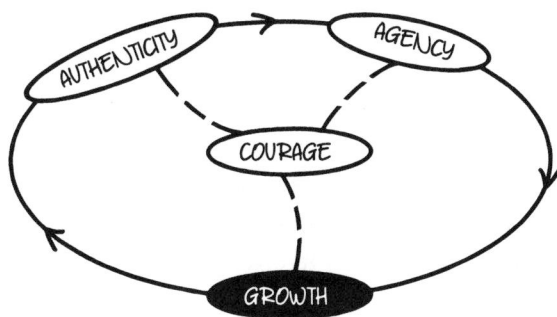

On paper, this sounds straightforward. But in practice, growth rarely follows a straight path. More often, it arrives uninvited—wrapped in discomfort, forcing us to question not just our choices but our values. For Mike, one such moment arrived unexpectedly, bringing with it a lesson in humility.

Mike's Moment That Mattered: Fired

There are very few other moments that will humble you like being fired. Even more so when you have, for the vast majority of your life, been the kid that is the rule follower, the try-hard kid, the one who isn't always the most talented, but the one that gets the "hustle" award. The one thing that no one ever questioned about my work was whether or not I did enough. So when I say that I wasn't truly prepared for the moment when I was fired from Tesla for my performance, or lack thereof, I mean it.

Now you are probably saying to yourself, "Mike, didn't you tell that intern that you approached everything like you were already dead and that it wouldn't matter if you got fired or not?"

Yeah, I said that, and I meant it. I had experienced years of layoffs, departmental reorganizations, and leadership changes (many of which involved the leader being fired). But what I had found to be true as well was that when you worked hard and gave everything that you had, it typically worked out. At least it had for me up until that point. It was who I was, too, the hardworking, hustle-award-winning leader. It was almost like the notion I might make it out alive crept into the back of my mind. I felt like there was some safety and goodwill based on how I showed up. I was wrong in the end. Maybe it was just arrogance that somehow, I was the exception. Like I said, humbling.

This story picks up right where my last Moment That Mattered left off. In late November 2021, I stepped into a role as "chief of staff" for our HR executive—a position I thought would allow me to align my values with meaningful work. But as events unfolded, I began to realize how quickly tension can shift mountains, exposing vulnerabilities and challenging even the most steadfast identities. As part of that role, I took on the task of leading a task force to retrain every people leader in the company on the value of respect in the workplace, their expectations as a leader, and the potential consequences if they failed to meet those expectations. The program had roughly a six-week timeframe where about thirty thousand people leaders within the company needed to attend a live, facilitator-led training session on the topic. Not a recording, not a course pushed to them on the computer, a live training. I had a great team of HR professionals supporting me in delivering the training, but the task was monumental. I basically lived in one of the factories for those six weeks, often delivering eight training sessions a day. By the time Christmas rolled around, I was burned out. Crispy.

A funny thing happened right as the program started. The leader whom I was meant to be supporting as their chief of staff left the company in the first week I was in the role. It was sudden, and I didn't have any time to really process it, as I was neck-deep in the leader training program. When I had run the calculus for the risks in the role, this was not one of the factors that I had considered. I was meant to help bring together the programs to bring her leadership vision to life, and now that leadership and vision were gone. The calculus changed, and I could feel a new tension start to creep in.

The transition was uncertain, with an interim leader taking on the role. This is where I began to feel the signs that my time was coming to an end. By the end of December, that new leader went silent on me for weeks. If you have ever been in a situation where you have been avoided by your leader, it is a telltale sign that something is wrong. I could barely get them to respond to an email, let alone talk to me in person. I didn't have any time to get to know them because of the training program. Each day brought a growing ache in my chest—a tightness that felt like a storm brewing just beneath the surface. It wasn't just the stress of the program; it was the creeping realization that my footing as a leader was slipping. That dissonance—between the values I held and the silence from my new leader—brought that new tension to the forefront, a constant hum of anxiety, a signal that something profound was about to shift. I've come to understand that tightness was likely low-level anxiety attacks; they happened constantly for weeks.

Now I wasn't totally caught off guard. Because I saw the signs, I had lined up a new job, looking for leadership and an organization that would help bring me out of the dark at Tesla. I wanted to be able to land with some forward momentum. I knew there was always a bit of a hangover when folks left the organization, so it was important to me that if this was to be my time, I could use it to make the right next step. So my exit plan was prepared, and I waited.

Confused yet? How could I be caught off guard if I saw the signs, if I had a plan, and I had been working as if I were already dead? Well, let me tell you why I was not prepared for what that moment meant to me.

It happened on a Friday afternoon in February of 2022, and my parents were visiting. I had a random calendar invite from my leader and our HR partner. I was in the car with my dad when the calendar invite came through, and all I could think was, "Just keep it together." The anxiety I felt over that eight weeks came to a crescendo, and I felt like I had just been dipped into an ice bath. It was hard to breathe. It was hard to talk.

We pulled into the driveway, and I locked myself in my office until the meeting.

When the time came to face the moment, I couldn't muster the courage to turn on my video for the call. Neither did they. They gave the news and explained it was due to "my performance" on a different project that had been assigned to me by the leader that left right as I started a role. A project that had been sidelined by the massive training effort. They were right; I hadn't worked on the project, but what took me by surprise was the total disregard for what I had done when it came time for the decision to fire me. That broke something in me that it took a very long time to discover. At the time, I didn't have the fight left in me to battle back, and with the other role in my pocket, I took it on the chin.

Immediately after the call, I called Kristen to tell her the news. I was in shock, looking back, but all I could do was think to tell her and then call my former direct reports. Too often leaders completely disappeared, never to be heard from again, and I didn't want those folks to have to wonder. I was honest about what happened but immediately turned the focus to my team to ensure they were OK.

I was deflecting, of course, because I couldn't process the moment myself.

Mostly, I felt ashamed. Shame and self-doubt that came from a fundamental break from the identity that I had as a hardworking, by-the-book type of leader, and what I had just been told was the reason for my exit. It didn't matter whether I felt like the reason was justified. That part of my identity was fundamental to who I was as a person, and in that moment that foundation was completely wiped out. Fire me because you don't like me, or because my role is being eliminated or because I didn't have a place under the new leadership. Fine. I'll deal with that. But to say that reason was performance related cut to the bone. It was like all the work that I had put into the organization and to prepare myself for that moment was stripped back to reveal something raw.

Worst yet, my parents were visiting, and I would have to try to carry on that day and in the visit because they knew me as the try-hard, straight-A student who never broke the rules. Carry on for two little boys who only knew me as their dad who worked at a company that was changing the world. Carry on for my wife, who knew me to my core and knew this would tear me apart. I put on a brave face for the rest of the weekend and tried to stuff the emotions as far down as I could.

Reflecting on this moment now, I realize how vital it is for leaders to confront the outcomes of difficult experiences head-on. My story highlights a truth we often avoid: growth begins when we stop running from the discomfort of our failures and instead embrace their lessons. I picked this story to share because it is a moment that most all of us fear. But I share this story, too, because while I had a plan and lived by what I thought was right, both who I was as a leader and what I did, I still got knocked on my ass by the moment. It lingered with me, too, because I didn't fully take time to appreciate what had happened and adapt from that situation. What I experienced wasn't about being a leader but finding the right place to address this core loss of my identity.

The very nature of my identity was challenged and questioned. I had internalized it all—hardworking, by-the-book, try-hard, straight-A, rule following. I couldn't reconcile that moment that shook my identity so violently. I thought that the next job was going to fix all my problems because I thought I could just ignore what the experience meant to me. A new team, a new role, new leadership—all could magically make it better. I could show up as the same old hardworking Mike, and everything would just go back to normal.

Shocker—it didn't go back to normal.

And that doesn't sound like growth, does it? The truth is, I wasn't ready for growth. At the time, I didn't realize it, but I needed to grieve and heal before anything else. I had avoided the difficult emotions, thinking they would pass on their own, but they didn't. I needed to face those feelings head-on, find meaning in the experience, and let it shape me. Without doing that, I was stuck, unable to move forward or learn from the situation. Growth doesn't happen by ignoring what hurts—it happens when you allow yourself to feel, reflect, and process what's truly going on. Without engaging in growth, I couldn't move forward in The Agency Loop; growth was the next step I had to embrace to keep progressing.

Growth Defined

Throughout this book, we've shared our Moments That Mattered—key experiences that revealed our courage. These moments highlighted the power of agency and how The Agency Loop helped us harness and channel that courage. While we could have called them reflections or left them out entirely, we intentionally chose to call them Moments That Mattered because they hold deep meaning and have shaped the leaders we've become.

We all have experiences that influence us and our careers, but Moments That Matter stand apart. It's not just about the experience itself, but about the meaning you derive from it. What creates the tension is how we choose to interpret those moments. Growth emerges from these experiences when you recognize the tension, feel it, and decide to take action.

When we shared that Mike wasn't ready to grow from his experience, it meant he wasn't yet ready to reflect on the meaning of that moment and how it shaped his values and identity. Growth happens when leaders are willing to confront that meaning, process it, and use it as a foundation to move forward.

Growth is a process, not a destination. In the context of The Agency Loop, growth is about becoming the person, the leader, you aspire to be. Becoming implies an active journey—a practice of reflection, courage, and intentionality. Growth asks leaders to intentionally reflect on their experiences and to learn from them. This requires holding space to examine the gap between expected outcomes and actual outcomes when acting with agency. In this reflective process, leaders anchor themselves in courage and two essential elements of growth: appreciation for their journey and adaptability for their next steps.

Growth, at its core, is the intentional practice of appreciating experiences and learning to adapt leadership through the value derived from those experiences. We define growth as the ability to learn, adapt, and evolve through your experiences.

It's not always easy; it takes courage to face the discomfort of holding up the mirror to one's actions. Leaders must wrestle with the realization that some values or identities they've long held may no longer serve them. Growth requires asking tough questions: Do the things I believe made me who I am still hold true in the outcomes of my actions?

Courage is the cornerstone of growth, as it enables leaders to confront pain and fear—emotions deeply rooted in the neural pathways of the emotional brain.[2] Revisiting difficult experiences is uncomfortable, yet this act of reflection is where true growth begins. The process of reflection and adaptation often challenges leaders to realign their values with their actions—a process that demands courage and resolve.

While growth can happen incidentally—through observation or gradual exposure to new ideas—intentional growth as a leader is an ability, a skill to be practiced and refined. It's rooted in the mindset described by Carol Dweck, where growth becomes not just a conscious choice but a natural tendency. In her study of leaders who exemplified the growth mindset, she noted that each one recognized that "leadership is about growth and passion, not about brilliance."[3] Those leaders sought learning over time, confronting challenges and making progress. This mindset allows leaders to adapt and evolve with every experience.

Human beings, however, tend to avoid difficulty, optimizing

for comfort and efficiency rather than confronting challenges head-on. But to grow is to work through challenges, not around them. This is where resolve comes into play. Resolve is not static—it can waver or run out, much like a battery. Not all growth requires equal courage, but the practice of growth builds resilience and can compound over time.

The courage to grow also requires acknowledging that not every moment will bring clarity or perfect answers. Leadership involves navigating complex, unsolvable problems. The Agency Loop supports leaders in processing these challenges more efficiently, helping them apply past experiences to present dilemmas.

As leaders practice growth, they model intentionality and authenticity, influencing their teams through storytelling and behavioral actions that foster a culture of learning and adaptation. By embracing growth as a journey, leaders unlock their ability to guide others through the same process.

Growth is not a passive process; it's an act of courage and intention. In the next sections, we'll dive into the essential elements of growth—appreciation and adaptation—and explore how leaders can harness these practices to transform challenges into opportunities and setbacks into stepping stones.

Appreciation

Have you ever found yourself asking, When is enough, enough? Is it the next promotion? Or the next completed project? Or the next job? Or the next, or the next, and so on? The eternal search for more runs consistently through organizations that live and die by the next product release, expanding market share, or harvesting more value by the end of the next reporting period. Like we pointed out in the beginning of the chapter, organizations often spend far too little time recognizing employees for their accomplishments because the endless cycle of more continues.

Even we have fallen victim to it, the failure as a leader to take a beat and celebrate a win or to mourn a loss. The funny thing is that as employees and humans, we feel joy, excitement, pain, or sadness, but rarely are those given the time they need to truly form. Yet for all the retrospectives and feedback gathering, it is difficult for leaders to truly allow their teams the space to take in the lessons gathered. To be fair, leaders have multiple responsibilities, or even their own workstreams, that make it difficult to pause and appreciate the moment. And the wheel keeps turning, with the next deadline, next quarterly earnings report, or project tugging on your attention and pulling you away from the opportunity for growth. The point here is that courageous leaders create space for appreciation.

Appreciation gives a leader the permission to be in the moment of growth. To take full stock of the experience and the consequences of your actions and live through the moment. Of course this gives the opportunity to celebrate victories, wins, the good parts of the consequences, big and small. But this also gives permission to feel the failures and shortcomings. Appreciation allows for leaders to have the space and vulnerability to feel the emotions that come from the moments, and then begin to figure out what to do with those emotions. When the leader can do that, it can translate to the team the leader builds as well, giving those team members the same permission.

The *Merriam-Webster Dictionary* essentially says that appreciation is a mix of gratitude and awareness.[4] Gratitude not for the positive outcomes, but for the experience itself, the life you have lived, the opportunity you had to act with agency. Awareness for the impact that outcome had on you and the emotions you feel in that moment.

Appreciation is something more than the sum of those parts. Where gratitude and awareness fall short is the opportunity that appreciation provides to begin to make connections to where the experience connects to your values. We define appreciation as taking full stock of the experience and the consequences of your actions.

> **Tab This!**
>
> Appreciation is taking full stock of the experience and the consequences of your actions.

Appreciation implies that the experience has some value to you. The connection of that experience to your values and identities, and the potential impact it has on those, begins to capture the full range of what appreciation can do for every leader who is in a growth moment.

We were awful at this for a very long time because in an environment of fear, you are always looking for the next opportunity to show value. Fear-based organizations don't give space for appreciation because they are always looking to maintain value and relevance (more about this in chapter 5). There is no value in what you did before, but rather in what you are going to do next. So the saying, "What have you done for me lately?" becomes "What are you doing for me today? And the next? And the next?" All because organizations that function on fear focus on maintaining control.

Now big caveat here: Not every organization that puts out a quarterly report or moves aggressively to launch products is a fear-based organization. But the ability to appreciate experiences often vanishes under fear-based leadership because the process of appreciation requires vulnerability and intention. If a leader is compelled to hide flaws in their decisions rather than learn from them, that leader is structurally limited in their growth. And while that may work in the short term to hit the next objective, it will stifle creativity and innovation in the long term.

How to Make Meaning from Your Moments

Appreciation provides a leader with the space to look back at decisions and actions, determine if there was a gap between the intended and experienced outcomes, and extract value—more specifically, the lessons learned and the meaning in the emotions experienced. The series of questions we call the Appreciation Questions will feel relatively straightforward if you've been reading the book cover to cover, as they reflect the steps in The Agency Loop. By engaging with these questions, you can turn reflection into actionable insights, fueling your growth as a courageous leader.

- What was the moment that mattered?
- What was the tension or dissonance in the experience?
- What were the expected/intended outcomes?
- What was the actual outcome?
- What were the consequences of the outcome?
- What emotions came from the experience?
- What do the outcomes and consequences mean *to* me?
- What do the outcomes and consequences mean *for* me?

The Appreciation Questions offer you a chance to reflect on your decisions and actions, helping you understand where there might have been a gap between your intentions and the outcomes you experienced. This process isn't just about looking back at what went wrong—it's about acknowledging the emotions tied to those moments and uncovering the lessons they hold. We've all faced situations where our best intentions didn't lead to the outcomes we expected. It's in those moments that we often find the most valuable insights. While reflection can be difficult, especially when timing and resolve present challenges, engaging with these questions allows you to turn tension into opportunities for growth, deepening your leadership and moving forward with clarity and purpose.

Timing and Capacity for Appreciation

If you are wondering how long it took Mike to get to the point where he was ready to truly start this appreciation process, it was likely longer than you think. It wasn't until we began writing this book—well over two years later—that he was able to fully process the moment using the questions we outlined above. Timing matters, even to us.

This brings up an important question: When is the right time to begin the process of appreciation? How do we define the right timing? Much like our decision-making process in agency, the right time for a leader to engage in appreciation depends on their personal situation and mental state.

Psychologist Abraham Maslow, known for his hierarchy of needs, believed that people can only focus on deeper thinking and self-growth when their basic needs—like safety and stability—are met. In *Motivation and Personality*, he explained that before someone can reach their full potential (a stage he called self-actualization), they must first feel secure in their environment. If a leader is dealing with uncertainty or stress, they may not yet be in the right mental space to reflect on past experiences in a meaningful way.[5]

Similarly, psychiatrist Elisabeth Kübler-Ross, known for her five stages of grief, believed that people process difficult experiences in stages, moving from denial to eventual acceptance. She argued that true reflection and growth can't happen until a person reaches the final stage—acceptance—where they are able to look at an experience with more clarity and less emotional weight.

In the same way, a leader may not be ready to fully process a challenging moment right away. If they are still in the middle of frustration, denial, or uncertainty, forcing appreciation may feel impossible. Kübler-Ross's model suggests that leaders need time to emotionally work through an experience before they can step back and truly appreciate what they've learned from it.[6]

Both Kübler-Ross and Maslow emphasize the importance of readiness—whether it's about grief or personal growth, people need the right mental and emotional foundation before they can engage in deep reflection. It's helpful to think in terms of temporal proximity, or the time that has passed since the experience happened to talk about readiness.

Table 4.1. Appreciation in Terms of Temporal Proximity

Distance from Experience	Benefits	Challenges
Immediate Reflection	• Capture details that might fade over time, like specific emotions, tensions, and dynamics • Capture questions like "What just happened?" and "How am I feeling now?"	• Emotional intensity may cloud judgment • Immediate processing could be focused too heavily on the emotions rather than actionable, long-term growth
Delayed Reflection	• Gives space for emotions like anger, shame, and sadness to dissipate • Balanced perspective of outcomes, consequences, and personal role • Provides time to incorporate broader themes	• Key details and nuances may begin to fade • Extended delay begins to teeter on avoidance

But what is that capacity to be ready to step into appreciation? It is helpful to think in terms of a leader's resolve.

Courage is the resolve to face fear, but we should remind you that resolve isn't constant—it's a resource that fluctuates over time. Because resolve is fluid, it affects the timing of when someone can process the impact of their experiences. They may not have it left in them at that time. This is why we describe growth as an ability: like any skill or muscle, it requires practice to build capacity, but it also needs rest. This creates cycles of resolve, where it builds up and can eventually be exhausted. Growth happens when you have enough resolve in the tank to do the work.

To illustrate this concept, we can turn to one of our favorite analogies—the aspen tree, which also serves as the basis for our company logo. Known for its resilience and adaptability (more on that later), the aspen tree thrives by developing a root system that supports growth. It waits for the right conditions in the environment before it sprouts and grows. Similarly, the roots may remain strong underground, preparing for the right moment. We see this as analogous to the conditions needed to support growth in leaders—having the right capacity and the supportive environment, such as psychological safety and self-compassion, to allow a leader to be ready to grow.

What makes aspens even more like leaders is that aspens grow as part of a colony, where trees may share root systems, connecting hundreds of trees over thousands of years. Just like aspens, leaders need a community of support, particularly when trying to make meaning from their experiences. Leaning on trusted colleagues to help reflect and provide perspective can aid in the process of appreciation and the exploration of the opportunity in adaptation.

What we offer here is a starting point for appreciation as well. Curiosity in courageous leadership is key to fully appreciating and understanding an experience. You have to be willing to ask questions that prompt exploration and understanding. When you explore your moments, you may not get appreciation right away. Your experience, your context, and your support system all impact when you are able to start the process of appreciation. It could take hours, days, or months. It is a courageous choice to sit with the discomfort of moments like the story at the beginning of this chapter. Remember to find balance; you don't need to rush it, but you don't want to avoid it, and it never hurts to find a leadership coach to lend a hand along the way.

Adaptation

We've always said feedback is a gift. While the process we outlined in appreciation is largely introspective in nature, it is feedback nonetheless. But in The Agency Loop, that feedback doesn't stop there. Adaptation is where we turn the meaning that we found into purposeful action. We think of adaptation as integrating the parts and pieces of our lessons learned.

> **Tab This!**
>
> Adaptation is integrating the parts
> and pieces of lessons learned.

Lessons learned come in many forms, and adaptation is about finding ways to carry those lessons forward in service of what truly matters to you. For our purposes, there isn't a step-by-step process in adaptation here. There are tons of great resources and practices like those in *Atomic Habits*, by James Clear,[7] or *The Power of Habit*, by Charles Duhigg.[8] Both have been influential in how we view adaptation and have their applications across leadership. Rather, our focus here is on nuances in adaptation that help connect your experience back to where we started in authenticity.

Adaptation in Small Steps

Adaptation is integrating the lessons learned into your leadership approach without losing sight of who you are and what matters most to you. Small steps in adaptation give you the opportunity to experiment and to pressure-test the changes you make. The key is to think of the experiment as a question rather than an answer. When you experiment as a leader, you are asking, If I do this new thing, implement a lesson learned, or make an adjustment, what will the outcome be? It changes the approach from certainty to exploration, giving space to find the right solution rather than stop at the first setback. And the right solution doesn't have to come the first time. When you make meaning of an experience, experiments help you test what that meaning could look like. Run the experiments with the purpose of getting back to this point again. Remember, experiments don't imply certainty but rather the exploration of opportunity.

We encourage leaders to approach experimentation by making small changes, focusing on 5 percent shifts at a time. We often work with Vanessa Shaw, an executive coach who works exclusively to build courageous leaders and founders, and she frames the 5 percent shift this way: What's the biggest small step you can take to move you one step closer to your goal?[9] The 5 percent shift is just that—it's the biggest small step. In chapter 2, Kristen shared her story of a 5 percent shift she used as the D&I leader navigating Tesla's response to the murder of George Floyd. A big change wouldn't have served her or Tesla. Instead, a 5 percent shift was effective. The goal is to stack those small changes over time, running the loop along the way, to move toward what matters most to you.

Growth and Loss

Experimentation and small steps give permission to explore what is possible and to test the lesson you learn in appreciation. But what happens when the results tell you that a value you held close or an identity you have isn't serving you anymore? What happens if you need to change that to move closer to a new vision of what matters most to you? What if, after the appreciation of your experience, you realize that what you thought mattered most ended up not being so important? Easy, right? Just toss that closely held value, belief, or identity in the bin and be on your way?

Well, no, it isn't that easy in practice. It's not easy because it is going to require you to change. Not just actions you take, but who you are as a leader. Humans at baseline are terrible at change because change invites an element of the unknown, whether positive or negative. This unknown stimulates a physiological response that functions in the same way as our fight-or-flight response. The underlying emotions are the fear of what is to come and the fear of the pain of losing what we know.

What makes it harder to change is that we don't spend enough time acknowledging what we are losing in the change. Often a value or identity that we have to say goodbye to has served us well in the past or is something that helped us get to where we are. In leaders this might look like the difficulty in transitioning from an individual contributor to management, leaving behind a value for feeling directly connected to the work instead of enabling their team to do their work. We have seen this in our consulting with veterans, helping them translate their strengths in their service into relatable stories for a corporate setting. And while we focused on helping identify what would continue to serve them, we made space to acknowledge, celebrate, and grieve the parts that did not serve them any longer.[10] And while in certain cases, these changes represent welcome steps toward what matters most, it can be difficult for leaders to accept the loss.

The struggle to accept loss and change brings us back to vulnerability and the need for self-compassion in the authenticity phase, both in mourning the loss and in building new identities and values from it. When we say that growth is about becoming the person you want to be, this process of adaptation is about intentionally integrating the lessons learned, not completely reinventing yourself as a leader.

The great part here is that you not only get to look at how your appreciation of the experience can move toward that shiny, authentic you, but you also get the chance to question: Is this even who I am anymore, or is there something even more that I haven't thought of? Often the path toward that ideal you is not clear. Adaptation represents the small steps you take from the lessons you learn to get to that ideal. Courage is needed, though, because you aren't going to know the way. This is why we talk in terms of a leader's life as a journey. The concept of a journey implies that there will always be some unknown with the next steps, just like life. This isn't a road map; rather, adaptation gives you the next step on your journey.

Closing the Loop: A Courageous Leadership Journey, Not a Destination

The Agency Loop provides courageous leaders with a practice to navigate the gap between their values and their environment through three interconnected phases: authenticity, agency, and growth. However, this process isn't a rigid, linear path, and neither is leadership. Leadership is not about reaching a final destination—it's about an ongoing journey of continuous evolution.

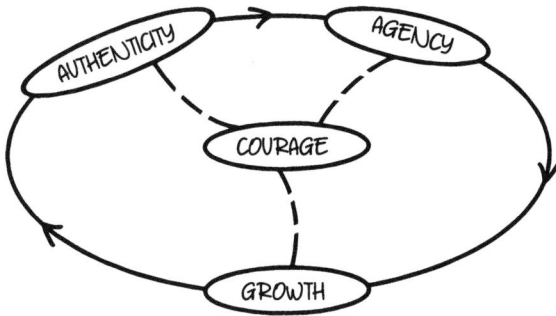

Remember where we have traveled in this journey:

- Authenticity: your ability to align who you are with how you show up in the world
- Agency: your ability to make intentional decisions based on your values
- Growth: your ability to learn, adapt, and evolve through your experiences

Each cycle of the loop doesn't end after the growth phase. Instead, it serves as the foundation for the next cycle, enabling leaders to integrate lessons learned while preparing to face future challenges. Leaders may revisit phases, experience them concurrently, or encounter multiple moments of tension that require them to navigate the loop at different levels.

After each cycle, we are not the same leader we were before. What we once considered authentic may no longer reflect who we are, because we have grown and changed. Growth isn't about endlessly repeating the same cycle—it's about evolving and elevating as we move forward in our journey.

A Spiral, Not a Closed Loop

At first, we struggled with the idea of a loop. We didn't want to suggest that leadership development was just an endless repetition of the same cycle, like a mouse on a wheel. The reality is far more dynamic. The journey matters because it reflects the evolution of our leadership path over time.

Rather than thinking of it as a loop, we began to see it as a spiral—one that builds upon itself. Each cycle deepens our ability to lead with authenticity, agency, and courage. With each iteration, we become more adept at recognizing tension, navigating uncertainty, and making decisions rooted in our values. Most importantly, courage grows over time.

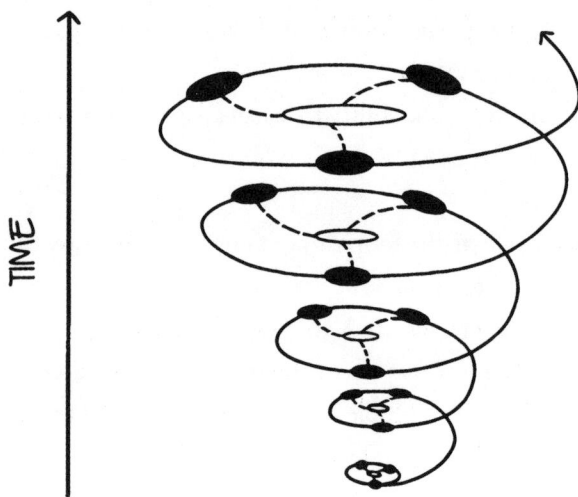

Growth isn't symmetrical or constant. Just like aspen trees need the right conditions to thrive, leaders must create environments that foster learning and resilience. But the goal isn't to escape the loop—it's to move through it with greater ease and clarity over time.

For us, it took years to even recognize that the loop existed. But once we did, it became a core part of our leadership practice. That's why we started The Agency Initiative—to help leaders recognize the power of agency and use it to shape their workplaces, their teams, and their impact.

Mike's Moment That Mattered: Closing This Loop

It would have been easy to tell a different story. One that felt safer, one that didn't require revisiting the pain of getting fired. But if we're talking about closing the loop, then I have to talk about this—because it was one of the hardest loops I've had to close.

For a year after I left Tesla, my commute took me past the factory twice a day. Every morning and every evening, I was forced to relive that moment. A thousand tiny reminders. Death by a thousand cuts. Brutal, huh?

Yet I didn't talk about it—not with colleagues, not with friends, not even with the people closest to me. I bottled it up like a French press jammed too far down, letting the pressure build. It was a form of self-preservation, or at least that's what I told myself. In reality, I felt ashamed.

Ashamed, because I knew that silence wasn't the way through it.

Ashamed, because in that silence I created distance from the people who mattered most.

Ashamed, because even though others would have told me this moment didn't define me, I still had to figure that out for myself.

But there was another layer of shame—one I didn't admit to myself for a long time. I knew I wasn't being the kind of leader I tell others to be.

I talk about courageous leadership. About speaking up. About leading by example, even when it's hard. But here I was, doing the opposite. Avoiding the conversation. Letting fear keep me from stepping into the kind of leader I knew I wanted to be.

That realization was almost worse than the event itself. Because I wasn't just letting myself down—I was failing to embody the kind of leadership I believed in.

And underneath all of that, there was something even deeper: the loss of identity.

I had always been the kid who tried the hardest. The one who outworked everyone. That was how I measured my worth—not by talent, not by luck, but by effort. And then, in one moment, it felt like that identity had been stripped away. Getting fired from Tesla felt like a gut punch to that part of me. Had all that effort meant nothing? Had I just been fooling myself into thinking that hard work was enough? For a long time, I couldn't talk about it. But I stayed curious about it. I kept searching for meaning, even when I didn't have the words.

And then Kristen and I started The Agency Initiative. This work gave me something I didn't even realize I needed—a way to bring the best parts of my experience at Tesla to life, instead of letting my exit define the whole story. It gave me a way to take that moment, strip away the shame, and replace it with meaning.

And that's when I realized something even more powerful: getting fired didn't take away my identity as someone who works hard. My employer didn't get to own that part of me unconditionally. I got to define what hard work meant. Hard work wasn't about proving my worth to a company. It wasn't about working myself to the edge of burnout for someone else's bottom line. It was about choosing where I put my energy and whom I put it toward.

And that is what closing the loop is really about.

The Work Never Ends—and That's the Point

We use the term "closing the loop" to represent completing a cycle, but in truth, the loop never truly closes—just as the leadership journey never ends. Each cycle may feel like a moment of completion, but it's really just a stepping stone in an ongoing process of reinvention, experimentation and learning. The loop doesn't stop; it keeps evolving, just as leadership does.

So what happens next? Simple: Run the loop again.

Fear isn't going anywhere. Uncertainty, failure, rejection, impostor syndrome, external pressures—they all show up, again and again, in different forms. In the second half of the book, we'll talk about three of the biggest uncertainties shaping leadership and stoking fear today: the deprioritization of DEI, political and social polarization, and the rapid rise of innovation. These aren't abstract ideas; they are real forces that keep leaders stuck, questioning themselves, and hesitating when action is needed.

But here's what we've learned: fear isn't the enemy of courageous leadership—it's the call to courage.

The mistake most leaders make is seeing fear as a signal to stop. But what if we flipped that? What if, instead of seeing fear as the thing that holds us back, we saw it as the doorway to action?

Fear exists where there's something at stake. And if something is at stake, that means there's an opportunity. An invitation to take the biggest small, 5 percent step forward, toward courage.

Courage isn't about eliminating fear. It's about identifying where you have agency and making a choice, even in the presence of fear. It's about recognizing that, yes, the fear is real—but so is the opportunity on the other side of it. And the leaders who move forward aren't the ones who wait for fear to disappear. They're the ones who see the opening and take the next step anyway.

Leadership isn't about closing a loop—it's about completing one and preparing for the next. Each pass builds strength, making the next challenge just a little easier to navigate. And that's the shift.

We don't avoid fear. We move through it—not by waiting for certainty, but by choosing agency, one step at a time.

The loop isn't just a process. It's a practice.

Make It Matter: Growth

Use this exercise below to help you identify where you are and the next steps to take in your journey toward courageous leadership—because it only matters if you Make It Matter.

Making Meaning from Experience

Growth often comes from moments of tension—times when your expectations and reality don't quite match. These moments challenge you, but they also shape the leader you are becoming.

In this exercise, you'll reflect on a Moment That Mattered in your leadership journey and explore what it means for you moving forward.

Think of a time when you faced a challenge or unexpected change in your leadership. Maybe it was a setback, a tough decision, or a shift in how you saw yourself.

Explore What Happened

- What was the situation? (Briefly describe it.)
- What made it challenging? (What tension or discomfort did you feel?)

- What did you expect to happen? (What outcome were you hoping for?)
- What actually happened? (How did things unfold?)
- What were the consequences? (What changed for you afterward?)
- How did you feel throughout the process? (What emotions did you experience?)

Take a Step Back

- What did you learn about yourself as a leader?
- How has this experience shaped the way you lead today?
- Is there a part of this lesson you haven't fully appreciated yet?
- What, if anything, do you need to let go of to move forward?

Apply It Now—the 5 Percent More Courageous Approach

- What's one way you can use this lesson in your leadership this week?

PART 2

COURAGEOUS LEADERSHIP IN UNCERTAIN TIMES

Part 1 of this book was a call to courage—an invitation to step into leadership with intention through the application of The Agency Loop. We explored how this framework helps leaders navigate uncertainty by aligning their values, decisions, and actions in ways that foster trust, resilience, and curiosity.

Now in part 2, we turn our focus to the real-world fears and uncertainties that challenge leaders every day. These moments of tension can cloud judgment, stall growth, and test leadership effectiveness. We'll examine three major forces reshaping the workplace: the deprioritization of DEI, political and social polarization, and the rise of innovation and artificial intelligence. Each of these presents a unique source of uncertainty—pushing leaders to confront complexity, make bold choices, and stay grounded in their values.

Left unchecked, these tensions don't just slow progress; they can derail leadership altogether. Each chapter will also introduce a durable skill—a tool you can use to lead with confidence, clarity, and purpose in the face of fear.

As you move through part 2, you'll encounter real-world challenges that require both thoughtful reflection and practical application. To support you in navigating these challenges, we've included an Additional Resources section at the end of the book, featuring tools, exercises, and case studies designed to deepen your understanding and help you apply the concepts from The Agency Loop in your leadership journey. These resources will provide the practical support you need to continue growing with intention and confidence.

FEAR IS THE MIND-KILLER

CHAPTER 5

Fear and Uncertainty

In recent years, uncertainty has become a constant in our lives, particularly within the context of leadership. If you think back to the early days of the COVID-19 pandemic, you might remember the profound sense of unpredictability that swept across the world. As lockdowns began, everything we knew about work, health, and even our daily routines was upended. The uncertainty felt overwhelming. Yet this initial wave of uncertainty didn't dissipate once the pandemic subsided—it only snowballed into new global challenges, each one compounding the previous. Over the past four years, we've transitioned from the pandemic to a contentious election, then from the election to inflation, and from inflation to AI. And now we find ourselves facing the combined forces of recession, inflation, and the result of another highly polarized election.

This isn't just a feeling—it's backed by data. The World Uncertainty Index, which tracks global uncertainty by analyzing country reports from the Economist Intelligence Unit, shows a sharp increase during the pandemic. Although it decreased in 2021, the index has been steadily rising again, approaching the levels seen during the height of the pandemic.[1]

All of this is underscored by a society in which civility is steadily declining, and trust in government institutions—the once highly trusted pillar of our social fabric—is eroding on a global scale. According to Edelman's Trust Barometer, confidence in government bodies continues to fall, creating a vacuum in which the public increasingly turns to other institutions—such as businesses—for stability and ethical guidance.[2] In this environment, workplaces are often expected to fill the gap, evolving not only into spaces for productivity but for fostering civility, trust, and a sense of community. Employers now face a dual responsibility: to support their employees' well-being and uphold values that were once the domain of societal institutions. This shift has placed an unprecedented burden on organizations, which are now expected to be bastions of integrity, respect, and inclusivity, all amid a landscape of political fragmentation and social uncertainty. Oh, yes, and turning a profit for shareholders.

Tab This!

We want to acknowledge that some individuals face an entirely different, and far more harrowing, type of uncertainty—one shaped by the devastating conflicts in regions like Ukraine, Gaza, Lebanon, and Sudan. These global crises create extreme instability and fear, a stark contrast to the uncertainty many of us experience in the workplace. While the challenges in our work environments may differ in scale, they are no less real. The turbulence in the world today amplifies the uncertainty that has become an inescapable backdrop to our lives, adding to the complexity of navigating an already volatile global landscape.

Specifically, the deprioritization of DEI, political and social polarization, and rapid rise of innovation are reshaping industries, workplaces, and societies, each introducing its own set of challenges that amplify the uncertainty we face daily. The fear stemming from global uncertainties is driving leaders to act in ways that conflict with their values, as they feel immense pressure to guide their teams through these changes while maintaining stability and continuity. We will explore each of these three uncertainties in more detail in the next few chapters.

Leaders are not only facing pressure in the workplace due to these external forces—the pressure also creates internal conflict. This fear, whether recognized as such or not, is pervasive. It seeps into their psyche and the workplace, influencing how leaders make decisions, how they interact with their teams, and how they navigate challenges. This fear—of failure, the unknown, losing control, and others—drives leaders to act defensively, stifling creativity and risk-taking, and creating environments where employees feel disconnected and disengaged. Fear begets fear. All too often it drives leaders to rely on fear-based leadership. While a natural response to uncertainty, it only deepens the cycle, trapping leaders and their teams in a constant loop of stress, avoidance, and missed opportunities.

For many leaders, uncertainty isn't just a theoretical challenge— it manifests in unexpected moments that test their resolve. These moments can arrive out of nowhere, catching leaders off guard and forcing them to confront fear and decision-making in real time.

Mike's Moment That Mattered: The Calendar Hold

These days nothing calls into question your footing quite like an impromptu calendar hold set for thirty minutes from the moment you receive it (for good reason, as we saw in chapter 4). It was early 2020, and I received just such a hold after only about six months in my new role leading the performance management program for the company. To make it worse, I was on a work trip at our California-based production facility and away from my team.

I'd been here before—where the surprise calendar invite slammed into my inbox with some version of the title "Quick Sync" or "HR Update."

The fear and corporate millennial anxiety rushed over me like a wave. I immediately started inventorying the potential reasons for the meeting. I had been working on a challenging new program to bring skills-based pay and career progression to line-side production workers. *Had I pushed too far too fast? Whom had I pissed off? Was I about to meet my end at the company like I had seen so many others go?*

As a veteran to this process, my learned reaction was to look at the meeting invitees. If I was the only one, then I knew what it meant for me. I wasn't the only one listed. My entire team was invited, along with others from the HR organization.

A quick flash of relief came over me. At least I knew it wasn't my time. But what then? My mind raced—a layoff or another reorganization? We'd had so many over the past few years that the thought of another made my stomach turn. I looked at the invite again and noticed my current manager wasn't on the meeting invitation. That was all that I needed to know to recognize what this call was about.

I spent the next thirty minutes cycling between possibilities, only to have my assumption confirmed. In the call, the HR business partner shared that *effective immediately*, my manager was no longer with the company. That person had been my sixth boss in three years, so I had grown immune to the shock of the news of my leaders' exits. *But what did that mean for the team?* This team, my peers and I, had only been together for three months—an amalgamation of teams cobbled together after a previous reorg.

Who would be the next one to take over leading that team? Corporate battlefield promotions were the norm, with the next most senior person or the biggest flight risk offered the job on the spot. What came next in this instance was unexpected. There was no plan for what was going to happen with the team. No strategy, no road map, no next steps. Not even a battlefield promotion.

Here is the kicker: two weeks later, life ground to a halt, and the whole country shut down. COVID-19 lockdowns kicked into effect, and for what seemed like an eternity, not only did I question whether I was going to have a purpose or role at work, but I also questioned if my family was going to live. I had just found out that I was going to be a father again, that my three-year-old would now be home indefinitely, and that my wife was going to have to go to work in a pediatric ER where undoubtedly, she would be exposed to the virus while in the early stages of pregnancy.

We were placed into a holding organization for the next two months while HR leadership determined the next steps for the org. I was in total limbo, glued to the TV and the computer screen, hanging on to some semblance of a life that had been flipped upside down in an instant. Fear was a constant companion at home and at work. Driven by the pandemic and compounded by the limited transparency from my leaders, it permeated my life and consumed every ounce of energy I had to give.

I knew I didn't want to keep living in fear, and if I was feeling that way, the team was feeling it too. I couldn't give them any answers, but I could give them a place to be real. And while I wasn't the official leader, I knew that I needed to do something to bring stability to the organization between the moments of uncertainty and fear. I needed to have the courage to do something to help us all find moments for release—by creating space for a quick check-in on a colleague, holding the space to air concern or mourn loss, or saying out loud, "I don't know what is next, but we'll face it together."

I knew all of the things that I wished that I had from a leader at the time and turned that into a driving force behind how I would show up. I didn't want to be a leader who was paralyzed by uncertainty, even though I doubted the way forward. I needed to genuinely care about my team. And in a company where fear-based leadership was the norm, I realized that bar was low. I didn't have to perform heroics (there was plenty of that to hear about on the news) to have an impact on my team. I found that it was the little things that mattered—showing up in the small moments and staying true to my values made all the difference for the team.

It would be easy for me to look back on those moments and romanticize how brave my team was at the time. But there was nothing romantic or extraordinary about our courage. What those leaderless months at the beginning of COVID-19 taught me, though, is that while none of us had control over what would happen to the team, or our families, or the country for that matter, we could control how we acted and showed up for each other.

My experience demonstrates a powerful truth: while leaders cannot control all the uncertainty around them, we can control how we respond to it. In that moment, I chose to show vulnerability, offer a sense of stability, and lean into small acts of courage. By doing so, I didn't just navigate my own fear and uncertainty—I set the tone for other leaders around me. Leadership in times of crisis isn't about having all the answers; it's about refusing to succumb to the fear and creating an environment where people feel safe to face uncertainty together.

This experience is a stark example of how uncertainty breeds fear in real time—both driven by global events and internal anxieties. The anxiety and hesitation I felt, not knowing what the future would hold for my team, are emotions that many leaders can relate to. When faced with situations that defy our control, fear often takes over—clouding judgment and stifling the ability to lead with clarity. This fear, whether acknowledged or not, doesn't just stay in the leader's mind—it begins to shape how they lead and how their teams respond. The very same fear that initially paralyzed me in the team's moment of crisis is the driving force behind many of the behaviors we see in leadership today.

The Evolution of Fear in Leadership: From Organizational to Internal Control

The fear that stems from uncertainty can create a cycle. Instead of confronting it with clarity and intention, leaders may avoid or suppress it, hoping it will go away on its own. But this avoidance doesn't solve the problem. It intensifies it, leading to more anxiety, more defensiveness, and more fear-based decisions. This cycle only deepens as leaders begin to see control and rigidity as their only tools for managing uncertainty, ultimately creating an environment where progress is stalled, innovation is suppressed, and employees feel disengaged.

Uncertainty is the seed, but fear is what grows from it—shaping how leaders behave, how they engage with their teams, and how they navigate challenges. Recognizing this transformation is the first step in breaking the cycle of fear and embracing the courage needed to lead through uncertainty.

It's one thing to face and react to uncertain situations, but it's another to internalize that uncertainty and let it shape our actions and decisions. As leaders, we find that the inability to predict outcomes can trigger an emotional reaction that paralyzes us. When this happens, it's no longer just about the unknown; it's about the fear of how that unknown will impact us, our teams, and the organization. This fear can take two forms: fear-driven leadership and fear-based leadership.

Fear-driven leadership emerges in response to external uncertainty. It's shaped by external pressures like economic challenges, market fluctuations, or organizational crises. Leaders who operate in this way react defensively to these circumstances, often making short-term decisions in an effort to protect the organization from perceived threats. While their actions may stem from valid concerns, fear-driven leaders risk prioritizing control over long-term stability and innovation, which can eventually undermine trust and collaboration.

On the other hand, fear-based leadership is deeply rooted in a leader's internal insecurities and fears. It arises from an emotional struggle where the leader's own anxieties about failure, loss of control, or their personal competence begin to drive their decisions. Fear-based leaders tend to cling to rigid control, avoid vulnerability, and suppress dissenting voices, creating environments where creativity and risk-taking are stifled. This internal fear doesn't just impact the leader—it spreads throughout the organization, influencing decisions, behaviors, and trust on a cultural level.

Whether triggered by external pressures or rooted in personal insecurities, fear becomes both a personal struggle and a cultural one. It seeps into the workplace, affecting leadership decisions, team dynamics, and ultimately, the overall organizational culture. In both cases, fear can create a toxic environment where growth, innovation, and trust are sacrificed in favor of control and short-term survival.

Fear-Driven Leadership

Fear-driven leadership, a response to external pressures, creates a sense of urgency and fear, prompting leaders to make decisions out of self-preservation or to protect their teams and organizations. Leaders in these situations may feel compelled to micromanage, tighten control, or implement immediate, short-term solutions to stabilize the situation.

While fear-driven leadership might feel like a necessary response to the external challenges at hand, it can inadvertently erode trust, creativity, and collaboration within the organization. In their efforts to manage uncertainty, fear-driven leaders may resort to rigid decision-making, limiting the autonomy of their teams and suppressing diverse perspectives. The focus on maintaining control can stifle innovation and lead to an environment where employees feel disengaged, undervalued, and hesitant to take risks.

As fear-driven behaviors take hold, the leader's external reaction to uncertainty can create a toxic cycle. Instead of encouraging adaptability, leaders may prioritize predictability and control, leading to burnout, disengagement, and missed opportunities for growth. When external uncertainty becomes the primary driver of leadership decisions, it risks turning the organization into a place where fear governs, rather than trust, collaboration, and innovation.

The more these fear-driven responses take hold, the more leaders may adopt rigid, controlling behaviors, believing that maintaining control is the only way to navigate the chaos. This shift from responding to external pressures to seeking internal control marks the transition from fear-driven leadership to fear-based leadership.

As fear becomes internalized, it shapes how leaders engage with their teams and how they perceive their role within the organization. Fear-based leaders, consumed by their own insecurities, begin to embrace authoritarian tactics as a way to regain control. This often leads to behaviors such as micromanagement, punitive measures, and the suppression of dissenting voices. Instead of fostering trust, curiosity, and resilience, fear-based leaders focus on stifling uncertainty through rigidity, creating an environment where failure is punished rather than viewed as an opportunity for growth.

When Fear-Driven and Fear-Based Leadership Collide

We're seeing a trend of amplifying fear and using it for personal gain on a global scale, where political and business leaders, like

President Donald Trump and Elon Musk, thrive in environments of fear and chaos and use it as a tool to consolidate power. These types of leaders rely heavily on authoritarian tactics, consolidating power and control by exploiting fear and division. Through charisma, persuasive power, and larger-than-life personas, they use outbursts of anger and veiled threats as tools to maintain dominance and silence dissent.[3] As this toxic behavior becomes normalized, it fuels a cycle of rising conflict and incivility across both workplaces and society. In doing so, they manipulate public fear, using it to strengthen their authority and influence.

This tsunami of fear-driven and fear-based leadership has begun to be normalized. Spreading rhetoric that is racist, sexist, homophobic, and xenophobic into our workplaces and communities has been mainstreamed. This collision not only increases tensions between people but deepens the sense of uncertainty in our everyday environments. Leaders today must navigate workplaces and communities that feel increasingly polarized, where fear and divisiveness threaten to undermine trust, collaboration, and progress.

We've witnessed leaders shrink in the face of this tsunami of fear, setting aside their values, staying silent in critical moments. We've witnessed leaders actively support harmful policies that fly in the face of their personal beliefs. Even more alarming is the impact of the trickle-down effect we see on young leaders who are socialized to emulate this authoritarian behavior as an acceptable and effective model for leadership. In many organizations, it takes real courage to resist this normalization, to stand firm in values when fear-driven leadership is internalized and spreading.

In most cases, leaders don't consciously choose a path of fear. Most leaders don't see what they are doing as employing fear tactics. Many are just trying to do the work and either take shortcuts or make assumptions about what is OK. We are willing to bet that some of you have used one or more of the tactics that we shared above, without even knowing, and that is OK. We've done it too; it wasn't a good look.

Kristen's Moment That Mattered: Don't Be a Jerk

I was on vacation when one of the managers on my team called. I felt the blood rush to my head the moment I hung up the phone. My anger surged, and I lost my composure. She called to tell me that the most junior members of her team had just briefed one of our most senior executives alone—and it didn't go well. The three of us had been working on a plan to bring this particular executive up to speed on a cross-functional DEI program we were engaged in with his team and make a few strategic requests for support. She had explicitly asked the team member to wait until we both returned to the office to finalize our approach before getting in front of the leader. But they didn't listen. Instead, they created their own briefing material, scheduled the meeting, and bombed the conversation—without my knowledge. Now our organization was at risk of losing the project altogether.

I immediately picked up the phone and called the team member (mistake #1). I greeted them with a sharp WTAF and a few other choice words (mistake #2). I was furious that they had gone behind my back and disappointed that the progress we'd made on the program was now in jeopardy because of a single, rushed meeting.

Underneath it all, I was scared—not just that we might lose the work, but because I knew how easily a poor performance in front of the wrong executive could lead to my team member's termination.

Most deeply, I felt betrayed. I had saved this team member from a reduction in force the year prior by hastily creating a role for them and convincing my boss that they would be an excellent performer and contribute positively in my organization. I'd trusted them and gone out on a limb for them. Now that trust felt completely shattered. And I let them know.

My team member didn't realize just how badly the call had gone. I explained the damage that had been done and the rapport that was lost in an instant. They got defensive and indignant. I saw red and hung up (mistake #3). Ultimately, we lost the work, and our relationship with our partner organization never recovered.

I cringe at that behavior now. I had seen it play out all the time around me, but this was the first time I really felt like I'd lost myself. In that moment of rage, I became the very thing I'd promised myself I wouldn't be—a jerk. It wasn't just about losing my temper; it was about losing sight of the leader I wanted to be.

I'd seen this pattern unfold around me countless times. People would hit their breaking point and tip over into authoritarian territory, as if the pressure, stress, and relentless expectations left them no choice. Fear and high stakes were constant, and despite the "Don't be a jerk" policy on paper, the culture told a different story. It was almost expected that people would snap, that harshness was part of what it meant to lead. Stress, poor mental and physical health, and intense demands created a pressure cooker, turning good leaders into something they never intended to be.

I already knew I was at a crossroads. Ironically, I had taken a vacation to give myself the mental space to decide whether I was truly going to resign in the coming months. This moment solidified my decision: I could stay and risk becoming someone I didn't recognize, someone hardened by the environment around me, or I could leave, preserve the values I wanted to lead by, and lead in a way that felt aligned with those same values. That moment was one of a final few wake-up calls—reminders that while I couldn't necessarily change the culture around me, I could still choose the kind of leader I wanted to be. Walking away wasn't just about escaping a toxic environment; it was about staying true to myself and committing to a different vision of leadership.

The Accidental Authoritarians

It would be easy to demonize every leader who uses the practices that we described in the previous section, but realistically the "Accidental Authoritarians," as we call them, often fall into cycles of behavior out of necessity or survival rather than nefarious intent. Far too often leaders whom we would categorize as Accidental Authoritarians aren't there because they have made that choice actively.

When we work with clients and leaders, we often share the message that we should assume positive intent when it comes to the actions of individuals and leaders within organizations. Most leaders typically don't wake up in the morning and say, "Today is the day I am going to be an asshole to my team" and create hostile, toxic, or dysfunctional work environments. At least we hope not. But a lot of leaders are paralyzed by fear. After all, these leaders are just people too. People who experience immense organizational pressure to perform, which can break down the practices of a functioning team over time. Those forces also cause leaders to continuously renegotiate the limits and boundaries they are willing to cross to achieve success. By getting curious and assuming positive intent, we can drop the judgment about the person's actions and get to the root of the problem the person is facing. (It's almost always fear.)

Organizational Responsibility and Individual Action

The good news (or bad, depending on how you want to look at it) is that the data backs the mounting pressure that managers feel to perform. The Deloitte Human Capital Trends 2024 report shows that 53 percent of managers say they are burned out at work.[4] Another report by Gallup shows that at least two-thirds of managers feel burned out at least some of the time, while quarter of leaders feel burned out often or always.[5] Mercer reported that managers bear the onus to "ensure their people leave work feeling good about their day and energized for tomorrow." The report goes on to show that managers are in the top five factors that cause employees to thrive in the workplace.[6] All of these signs point to the increasing exposure and pressure managers face in the workplace to perform, in particular middle managers who have responsibilities up and down within the hierarchies in the organization.

Fear. Additional data shows that managers may not be getting the skills they need to deal with the growing expectations. Gartner surveyed HR leaders, where they found that 75 percent of those surveyed reported that managers are overwhelmed with the expanding scope of their responsibilities. In the same report, only 23 percent of those same HR leaders surveyed say they are confident there are rising leaders who can meet the future needs of the organization. Leaders face increasing scope with decreasing preparedness, all the while expected to continue to increase team performance and drive organizational results.[7]

Fear. According to the Gartner report, 36 percent of surveyed respondents think their organizations' current leadership development programs are effective.[8] So if formal programs don't prepare leaders, where do leaders learn how to lead? Leaders learn from their experience and from the other leaders around them. When leaders see practices that feature threats, rebukes, and unwillingness to admit fault as common within an organization, that legitimizes those practices.

And more fear. We can't stop the uncertainties that compel fear-driven leadership, nor can we eliminate the external pressures that contribute to it. However, we can prepare ourselves for them. We can change how we respond to uncertainty, and instead of being overwhelmed by fear, we can choose courage over fear. By embracing frameworks like The Agency Loop, leaders can learn to navigate these challenges more effectively, making intentional decisions rooted in their values and fostering growth, trust, and resilience in their organizations.

In the remainder of the book, we will deep dive into the three key uncertainties—deprioritization of DEI, political and social polarization, and the rapid rise of innovation—and help leaders prepare to face them with courage and clarity.

COURAGE
PROTECTS
PROGRESS

CHAPTER 6

Courageous Leadership and Deprioritization of Diversity, Equity, and Inclusion

At the heart of today's deprioritization-of-DEI debate lies the intersection of three powerful forces: globalization and expansion, social pushback against inclusion, and evolving cultural dynamics and social relationships. Together, these forces create a self-perpetuating cycle. Globalization increases diversity, which necessitates inclusion and belonging, which amplifies cultural tensions and resistance, deepening the need for—and challenges to—intentional DEI efforts.

Globalization and Expansion

The workplace is diversifying across cultural, racial, and generational dimensions. By 2045, the US population is projected to become significantly more diverse, with substantial growth among Hispanic, Black, and Asian American communities. Simultaneously, the workforce is aging, with the number of workers fifty-five and older expected to grow three times faster than those aged twenty-five to fifty-four. As more generations work side by side—and people remain in the workforce well into their seventies—leaders face mounting challenges to foster environments that truly celebrate and include these varied perspectives.[1]

Globalization accelerates these shifts, requiring organizations to adapt to increasingly diverse teams and global markets. Cultural competence is essential for fostering innovation and success in this environment. However, the need for adaptability often conflicts with the pressures for standardization. Without intentional strategies, these tensions risk creating environments where cultural disconnect and exclusion take root, undermining the very diversity that drives progress.

Social Pushback against Inclusion

The 2020 murder of George Floyd galvanized corporations against systemic inequities, which resulted in a wave of corporate commitments to address the problems internally and within their communities. However, DEI efforts are now embroiled in a storm of resistance, misinformation, and political polarization. Organizations such as Target,[2] John Deere,[3] Harley-Davidson,[4] McDonald's,[5] Walmart,[6] Tractor Supply Co.,[7] and others have publicly scaled back their DEI initiatives under intense pressure from ideological groups and legal challenges. These entities argue that DEI initiatives risk legal liability or financial inefficiencies, emboldened by lawsuits alleging reverse discrimination or violations of antidiscrimination laws.

Corporate boards have been directly targeted by conservative think tanks advocating for the rollback of DEI policies, citing claims that they prioritize diversity over merit. These pressures have created a chilling effect, leading to the reduction of DEI efforts in some companies, while others—like Apple[8] and Costco[9]—have doubled down on their commitments. Costco's board of directors, for example, openly rejected calls to curtail DEI efforts, reaffirming their integral role in fostering innovation and market competitiveness.

This pushback reflects deeper societal and cultural divisions, fostering fear and uncertainty for leaders and employees navigating polarized workplaces. DEI professionals, in particular, have become scapegoats, bearing the brunt of criticism. Federal DEI initiatives face existential threats under intensified political pressures. Federal DEI teams and organizations were annihilated in the first few moments of the second Trump administration, as they had become targets of public and political ire, vilified in media and legislative arenas, while their essential contributions were diminished by blame and backlash.

Cultural Dynamics and Social Relationships

Amid the shifts of globalization and workplace diversification, another profound challenge has emerged: the erosion of organic, community-based connections that once naturally bridged differences. Activities like Little League baseball used to exemplify how diverse individuals came together, fostering trust and understanding. Today, the rise of travel sports, club leagues, and school choice has engineered more segregated communities, weakening these bonds.[10]

This fragmentation echoes in the workplace, where casual, meaningful interactions across diverse groups are diminishing. Social contact theory, or intergroup contact theory, offers a potential solution, emphasizing that sustained, positive interactions under conditions of equal status, shared goals, and institutional support can reduce biases and foster mutual respect.[11] Yet in a world increasingly shaped by curated social networks and echo chambers, such opportunities are rare.

For younger generations raised in these environments, the workplace may be their first exposure to bridging differences, especially in person. This presents both challenges and opportunities. On one hand, workplaces can become spaces where natural connections are rebuilt, fostering collaboration and trust. On the other, without intentional efforts to create these connections, workplaces risk reinforcing isolation and division.

Marc Dunkelman, in *The Vanishing Neighbor*, highlights the disappearance of "middle-ring" relationships—casual, everyday interactions between acquaintances that bridge social divides. These connections, crucial for exchanging diverse perspectives and building trust, are eroding as people self-select into like-minded communities. In the workplace, these casual conversations— across teams, roles, and departments—are vital for innovation and mutual growth but often feel foreign to those accustomed to curated networks.[12]

Building these connections in the workplace requires intentionality. Unlike curated social spaces, employees don't choose their teams. This lack of choice can create discomfort and opens the door for workplaces to become "corporate townships," where diverse individuals challenge each other's ideas and learn together. By fostering environments that embrace these dynamics, leaders can transform workplaces into spaces of understanding and inclusion, bridging the divides that fragmentation has deepened.

But we know old habits die screaming. As organizations and society confront deeply entrenched patterns of racism, sexism, and exclusion, resistance is both inevitable and often disruptive. This pushback, while painful, is a sign of progress—an upheaval that forces us to confront uncomfortable truths and opens the door to reimagining systems that embrace DEI. However, this period of transition brings significant fear and uncertainty for leaders, employees, and DEI practitioners alike, raising critical questions about how to navigate these challenges while fostering trust and inclusivity.

The Fear: Leading in a Lose-Lose Situation

In today's uncertain environment, leaders face an unsettling reality: navigating their company's deprioritization of DEI feels like being caught in a lose-lose situation. On one side, stepping back risks damaging trust, eroding morale, and compromising inclusivity. On the other, standing firm in support of DEI can provoke backlash, alienate stakeholders, or jeopardize careers. Compounding these challenges is the need to process what the company's retreat from DEI signifies on a broader level. Leaders must confront a complex web of fears that require careful navigation.

Fear of Stepping Back from DEI

Stepping back from DEI initiatives can erode the trust and goodwill leaders have worked hard to build. Employees may see this retreat as a betrayal of the company's values, leading to lower morale, disengagement, and higher turnover rates. Leaders also face personal conflict, as their decisions may clash with their principles, creating a sense of hypocrisy or internal dissonance. Externally, the company risks losing credibility with customers, investors, and partners who prioritize diversity and inclusion, potentially harming its reputation and market position.

Fear of Standing Firm in Support of DEI

Supporting DEI initiatives in a polarized climate comes with its own set of challenges. Leaders may face opposition from senior stakeholders or boards of directors who view these programs as politically charged or financially burdensome. They also risk career consequences, such as diminished opportunities or strained relationships with influential colleagues. Public backlash from political or ideological groups can further complicate matters, making it harder for leaders to advocate for inclusivity without fear of personal or professional repercussions.

Fear of What the Company's Deprioritization of DEI Signifies

Beyond immediate actions, leaders must wrestle with the broader implications of their organization's retreat from DEI. What does this shift reveal about the company's values and priorities? How will this decision affect its long-term culture and ability to foster innovation? Leaders may also question their alignment with the organization's direction, grappling with whether they can reconcile their personal values with the company's evolving stance. This reflection creates additional uncertainty, further amplifying the challenges of navigating this complex landscape.

The deprioritization of DEI commitments challenges leaders to balance diverse cultural perspectives while safeguarding inclusivity. The pressure to standardize practices risks diluting DEI efforts, leading to cultural disconnect and weakened belonging. As leaders face a lose-lose scenario of navigating polarization, they must reconcile their values with organizational priorities while fostering trust and inclusivity. In this fragmented landscape, their ability to address fears, rebuild connections, and sustain DEI principles will define the resilience and adaptability of their organizations.

The Answer: Courageous Leadership and Inclusion

Employees in environments like we've described above tend to feel a lack of personal control and influence in uncertain times. It is unreasonable—and ineffective—to expect employees to self-organize or solve systemic DEI issues on their own in these conditions. Out of desperation, they often turn to dominant leaders who they believe can restore their sense of control, but they don't want those leaders to be tyrannical.[13] They need courageous leaders.

Courageous leaders must step in to create a culture that fosters inclusion and belonging. Employees need leaders who set the tone, provide the structure, and champion the values that make a diverse workplace truly inclusive. Courageous leaders stand out because they don't rely on dominance or control. Instead, they create a culture where vulnerability is valued and trust is foundational, empowering employees to adapt rather than fear the unknown. By encouraging open communication and leading by example, courageous leaders show that adaptability and empathy can thrive, even amid uncertainty. Their ability to demonstrate trust, resilience, and curiosity amid the chaos reinforces those same qualities within the organization.

Courageous leaders can thrive in uncertainty. Courageous leaders also understand that fostering genuine connections is essential for inclusivity. They are intentional about creating spaces where social contact isn't just encouraged but is integral to the team's culture. To counteract the loss of organic connections, leaders need to be proactive in creating intentional opportunities for social contact to boost inclusion among their increasingly diverse teams. When leaders focus on fostering these intentional interactions, they create spaces for employees to experience the benefits of social contact—bridging cultural divides and building a resilient, inclusive workplace culture. For courageous leaders, creating intentional interactions isn't a checkbox exercise; it's a continuous commitment. They recognize that fostering inclusion requires consistent action and attention, embedding these practices into the organization's DNA.

Intentional interactions can also help reduce the cultural tensions that arise in fast-paced, diverse environments. By cultivating structured spaces where employees feel equal and supported, companies can bridge the gaps left by the loss of connections, bringing us closer to a "*Star Trek* future"—one where diversity is celebrated and inclusion is the norm. Courageous leaders make this *Star Trek* future possible by modeling inclusivity and fostering environments where diverse voices are valued and respected, setting the stage for a more resilient and adaptive workplace.

Promote Psychological Safety as a Durable Skill

In times of uncertainty, courageous leaders need practical skills to navigate complex challenges—especially today, with globalized workplaces and the shifting landscape of DEI. Cultivating psychological safety is one of the most powerful ways leaders can create an environment where all team members feel empowered to speak up, take risks, and bring their authentic selves to work, without fear of judgment or reprisal. Amy Edmondson, professor of leadership and management at Harvard Business School and an expert on psychological safety, defines it as a belief that one will not be penalized or humiliated for speaking up with ideas, questions, concerns, or mistakes.[14] This is particularly critical in diverse teams, where openness and understanding are essential for bridging cultural gaps and building a foundation of trust.

In a psychologically safe workplace, leaders transform uncertainty into an opportunity for growth and connection. By encouraging open dialogue, modeling vulnerability, admitting mistakes, and showing that it's OK to fail and learn, leaders actively foster a culture of inclusion. When leaders listen to diverse perspectives and ensure everyone feels heard, they lay the foundation for mutual respect and understanding. These actions create an environment where people feel safe to take risks, innovate, and contribute authentically, leading to more inclusive and adaptable teams.

By focusing on psychological safety as a durable skill and consistently practicing it, courageous leaders don't just navigate uncertainty; they intentionally cultivate an inclusive workplace where diverse voices are valued, respected, and empowered to drive long-term success. This creates the foundation for a more adaptable, innovative organization where every individual can thrive.

Courageous Leaders Can Act Now

In an era marked by globalization, cultural fragmentation, and a retreat from DEI commitments, courageous leaders like you are crucial in preserving the progress made over decades to create workplaces that celebrate diversity and foster inclusivity. While resistance to change and the retreat from DEI initiatives can feel disheartening, these moments offer a critical opportunity to be strategic about how we rebuild systems that work for everyone.

Courageous leaders recognize that advancing DEI is not just about managing change but about shaping the future of work with intentionality and resilience. By leaning into their core values and taking deliberate actions, they demonstrate that inclusivity is not an optional ideal but a foundational principle for thriving organizations.

In challenging moments, even small, intentional actions—such as fostering psychological safety, amplifying underrepresented voices, or addressing bias—can create meaningful change. Just acknowledging the challenges we face and creating space to discuss what it means to you and to your team is a powerful first step toward making meaningful change. These actions signal to teams and organizations that diversity, equity, and inclusion are not just priorities but essential pillars for innovation, collaboration, and sustainable success.

As the workplace continues to evolve, courageous leaders have the power to build environments where every voice is valued, and differences are seen as strengths. By stepping into this role with vision and purpose, you help shape workplaces where trust, equity, and inclusivity thrive, laying the foundation for a more just and resilient future.

Make It Matter

Growth and courageous leadership don't happen by accident—they come from intentional choices, practiced over time. The following actions offer practical ways to apply what you've learned, whether through small shifts in daily behavior or larger commitments that influence your organization.

Start where you are. Even a 5 percent shift in how you show up can create meaningful change.

Small Actions
(5 Percent More Courage—Start Today)

- Lift up voices that aren't being heard. If someone's idea gets overlooked in a meeting, bring it back into the conversation and give them credit.
- Make space for different perspectives. Pay attention to who speaks the most in discussions—pause and invite others in.
- Check in with a teammate. If someone seems disengaged or hesitant to share, ask how they're doing and what support they need.

Medium Actions
(Influencing Your Immediate Sphere—within Weeks)

- Look for where you have influence. Whether it's in team meetings, hiring decisions, or day-to-day culture, find small but meaningful ways to model inclusion.
- Start a conversation about psychological safety. Ask your team: "What helps you feel comfortable speaking up, and what gets in the way?"

- Get real feedback. Talk to colleagues with different backgrounds or experiences and ask, "What's working? What's not? What could I do differently?"

Big Actions
(Shaping Systems and Culture—Ongoing Commitment)

- Advocate for inclusive policies. Push for hiring practices, team norms, and policies that create real equity—not just performative change.
- Keep leadership engaged. Bring up inclusion in decision-making conversations, even when it's not the popular or easy thing to do.
- Support future leaders. Mentor or sponsor someone from an underrepresented background and help open doors they might not otherwise have access to.

COURAGE
BRIDGES
DIVIDES

CHAPTER 7

Courageous Leadership and Political and Social Polarization

Social and political polarization has reached unprecedented levels, affecting not only broader society but also the workplace. As ideological divides grow deeper, employees are increasingly influenced by the emotional and cultural climates surrounding political discussions. Issues such as the 2024 US presidential race, debates over DEI initiatives, and the evolving dynamics of remote and in-office work have introduced new layers of tension in workplace relationships. Employees are no longer just encountering differences of opinion; they're facing situations where opposing views are seen as not just divergent, but threatening. This growing polarization creates an environment where even minor differences of perspective can spark conflict and hostility. As a result, incivility—expressed through dismissive, disrespectful, or subtly antagonistic behaviors—becomes more prevalent, further eroding collaboration and trust.

Research from Professors Christine Porath and Christine Pearson, captured in their article "The Price of Incivility" for *Harvard Business Review*, highlights how incivility erodes trust, dampens morale, and diminishes productivity, often causing employees to withdraw or disengage.[1] The rising polarization in the workplace contributes significantly to this increase in incivility, with employees viewing colleagues' beliefs as not only different but oppositional. This view of differences creates a tense environment where incivility can thrive unchecked.

Polarization in the workplace is more than an internal challenge; it's increasingly spilling into the public view, creating reputational and operational challenges for organizations. The 2024 US presidential election serves as a prominent example, as many companies experienced a surge in workplace hostility around political discussions.[2] In response, human resource teams established guidelines for political expression, balancing free speech with civility and the need for workplace inclusion. However, leaders often fear that by establishing such guidelines, they may alienate employees who feel their voices are being suppressed or marginalized.

As polarization heightened, many organizations opted for political neutrality, avoiding public statements on potentially charged issues, and advising employees to focus on business operations rather than political commentary. This strategy aimed to prevent internal disputes from escalating and negatively affecting public perception. However, some employees expressed frustration with this stance, viewing neutrality as a suppression of their voices and values. Leaders may fear that taking a neutral stance could make them appear indifferent to important social issues, potentially alienating employees who expect the organization to reflect certain values.

According to a poll commissioned by Indeed and released by the Harris Poll, divisiveness has reached a point where nearly half of Americans under thirty-five have expressed a willingness to leave their jobs rather than work with colleagues or supervisors who hold opposing political views.[3] This trend highlights the depth of political polarization affecting workplace dynamics, with employees feeling increasingly uncomfortable around differing ideologies. Such sentiments underscore the importance of fostering an inclusive environment that manages ideological differences respectfully and constructively, but leaders face the challenge of walking a fine line between fostering unity and respecting individual expression.

Separate studies by international relations scholars and political scientists Rachel Kleinfeld[4] and Shanto Iyengar et al.[5] reveal how affective polarization, defined as negative feelings toward people who belong to opposing groups, leads individuals to distrust or even dislike others simply for identifying with opposing "camps," creating an "us versus them" mindset. In the workplace, these emotional divides hinder effective collaboration and fuel an atmosphere where incivility can flourish. False polarization, the mistaken belief that others' views are more extreme than they are, further widens this divide by exaggerating differences and reinforcing mistrust. Together, these dynamics create a cycle where perception becomes reality, making it even harder to build trust and bridge divides. Leaders must actively disrupt this cycle to create conditions for honest dialogue and productive teamwork.

The Impact of Polarization-Driven Incivility

The impact of polarization-driven incivility goes beyond individual discomfort; it has lasting effects on the entire organization. Left unchecked, incivility can escalate, leading to employee burnout, high turnover, and difficulty in attracting and retaining top talent. Organizations that gain a reputation for having a toxic or divisive culture may see these issues compound, harming morale and external perceptions, making it challenging to maintain a strong and resilient brand. Leaders may fear the potential for these reputational risks, knowing that unchecked polarization could tarnish the organization's public image and, let's be honest, the bottom line.

If not managed effectively, these tensions can erode team cohesion, trust, and productivity. Among various types of workplace conflict, incivility has become increasingly pressing, with US workers collectively witnessing over 190 million acts of incivility daily, according to the Society for Human Resource Management's 2024 Civility Index. This rise is linked to factors such as political viewpoints, social issues, generational gaps, and racial or ethnic differences. The shift to remote and hybrid work has further diminished informal interactions, leading to more misunderstandings and disrespect.[6]

We would argue even civility does not go far enough. Civility is the bare minimum—a baseline expectation for respectful interaction—but it does not guarantee inclusion. A workplace can be civil yet still leave individuals feeling excluded, unheard, or undervalued. Inclusion goes beyond mere politeness; it requires intentional efforts to ensure that every individual feels like they belong, that their perspectives matter, and that they have equitable opportunities to contribute and thrive. While civility mitigates harm, inclusion maximizes potential.

Furthermore, the connection between civility, inclusion, and psychological safety is essential to a high-performing workplace. Psychological safety allows employees to feel safe taking risks, sharing ideas, and engaging in open dialogue, which drives innovation and collective problem-solving. When leaders prioritize inclusion and at the very least civility, they create an environment where psychological safety can thrive, allowing team members to work through differences constructively. In organizations where DEI has been deprioritized, fostering psychological safety becomes even more critical, as it helps bridge the gaps created by diminished inclusion efforts and ensures that diverse perspectives remain integral to collaboration and innovation. Leaders, however, may fear that efforts to promote civility might inadvertently erode authority if employees misinterpret this openness as permissiveness or civility itself as a substitute for true inclusion. By addressing incivility and promoting a culture of respect and safety, organizations foster a workplace where team performance and engagement flourish, enabling them to meet challenges with resilience and agility.

The Fear: Us-versus-Them Mentality

While we often understand why employees struggle in polarized environments—fear of judgment, alienation, and the potential repercussions of being open about their beliefs—it's equally important to recognize the fears that leaders face when they step in to address these tensions.

Leaders can also face a complex array of fears when managing polarization within their teams. These fears can be divided into two main areas: concerns about what political and social polarization means for their role, and anxiety over what actions to take in response.

Fear of What Polarization Means

Leaders may fear that by taking a stance or addressing politically charged issues, they could alienate certain team members or come across as biased. This fear is centered on how their actions will be perceived—whether they will be viewed as favoring one side, compromising their neutrality, or unintentionally alienating those with differing viewpoints. This fear of being seen as partial or aligning with one "side" in an us-versus-them dynamic can cause leaders to shy away from addressing important issues altogether, inadvertently allowing polarization to deepen. Leaders may also worry about how their personal values align with their organization's stated values, mission and vision, especially in environments where employees already feel divided. Fearing backlash from senior leadership or stakeholders, they may unintentionally reinforce the us-versus-them dynamic by avoiding action.

Fear of Taking Action

The fear of taking action manifests when leaders are uncertain about how to respond effectively to political or social tensions without exacerbating them. Leaders may worry that taking actions like fostering civil discourse—engaging in respectful, open conversations where differing viewpoints are heard and valued—could be seen as stifling free speech, while allowing open dialogue might lead to escalating conflicts or disrespect. This tension—between promoting a culture of open dialogue and maintaining a respectful and cohesive environment—often leads to analysis paralysis. Leaders may avoid making any definitive decision because they fear doing more harm than good, further deepening divisions and creating an environment where tensions simmer below the surface without being addressed. This fear is often amplified by the potential reputational risks for both the leader and the organization, as any misstep can be magnified in a politically polarized climate.

Despite these fears, leaders have the unique opportunity to challenge the us-versus-them mentality by fostering inclusivity, civil discourse, and shared understanding. By stepping into discomfort, they can disrupt the adversarial dynamics and rebuild trust, demonstrating that courageous leadership can transform tension into progress.

The Answer: Courageous Leadership and Civil Discourse

Courageous leaders are intentional about embodying values like empathy, patience, and respect, especially when faced with conflict. Rather than avoiding disagreements, they view them as opportunities to engage and build stronger, more resilient teams. Civil discourse is not passive but an active practice of listening, understanding, and aligning with core values. Unlike broader organizational challenges like globalization or inclusion, conflict resolution often requires real-time interpersonal skills.

With societal polarization on the rise, tensions around political and social issues increasingly spill into workplace interactions, challenging cohesion and open communication. Employees may feel the need to "cover" or hide their perspectives to avoid judgment or conflict, which undermines authenticity and engagement. Leaders face a parallel challenge: balancing the need for civil discourse with the fear of alienating team members or appearing biased. These fears can lead to inaction, allowing tensions to simmer and potentially escalate into incivility—dismissive or disrespectful behaviors that erode trust, dampen morale, and hinder collaboration.

Courageous leaders confront these challenges by fostering an environment of inclusion, where clear expectations for civil discourse are set and diverse perspectives are valued. They foster open-mindedness on the team and encourage members to get curious instead of making snap judgments. Most importantly, when they hear something out of alignment with organizational values, they call it out. By addressing incivility head-on and modeling respectful dialogue, leaders create a culture where employees feel safe to express themselves authentically. This intentional approach not only helps maintain team cohesion but also reinforces psychological safety as a foundation for collaboration and innovation.[7]

These leaders recognize that fear often underlies conflict and can inhibit open communication and collaboration. By fostering psychological safety, they create an environment where team members feel empowered to express ideas and voice concerns without fear of judgment or retribution. This assurance is crucial for innovation and creativity, as employees are more likely to share diverse perspectives when they feel secure. In embracing their own vulnerabilities, leaders model for their teams the courage required to navigate polarization constructively.

In environments where incivility and polarization can quickly erode trust and morale, courageous leaders act decisively to prevent these behaviors from taking root. They address incivility head-on, setting clear expectations for respectful engagement and holding themselves and others accountable. By insisting on civility, as a bare minimum, and prioritizing inclusion and creating a psychologically safe space, courageous leaders enable their teams to navigate conflicts constructively, preserving cohesion and driving performance.

Through this intentional approach, courageous leaders bring us closer to a "*Star Trek* future," where collaboration thrives across differences, diverse voices contribute to shared goals, and collective growth is valued over individual divisions. In this future, conflict is not a threat to unity but a pathway to deeper understanding and mutual progress. Courageous leadership builds the groundwork for this vision—fostering a workplace where values-driven action, trust, and openness create lasting impact and move teams toward a truly inclusive, resilient culture.

Promote Civil Discourse as a Durable Skill

For courageous leaders, promoting civil discourse is a durable skill that transforms conflict into a constructive force within teams. Civil discourse—engaging in respectful, open conversations across differing perspectives—empowers leaders to guide their teams through challenges without allowing polarization or incivility to erode trust.

Contrary to common myths, incivility in the workplace is not merely the result of personality clashes or misunderstandings. Research shows that broader social polarization can fuel workplace tensions, with employees perceiving opposing viewpoints as threatening.[8] While creative tension—healthy, productive disagreement that fosters growth and understanding—can lead to positive dialogue and innovation, social polarization often escalates conflicts, making it harder to engage constructively. Courageous leaders recognize this difference and take steps to promote civil discourse, using it as a tool to engage with diverse perspectives, rather than avoiding or stifling disagreements.

In practice, promoting civil discourse starts with transparency—making it a goal or value of the organization. It involves setting clear expectations for respectful communication, providing training on active listening, and fostering an atmosphere where diverse viewpoints are valued rather than dismissed. Workplaces that successfully implement intentional inclusion programs and structured frameworks to support civil discourse demonstrate how clear behavioral norms can transform dynamics and reduce tensions. Leaders can adopt similar strategies to establish shared guidelines for interaction—such as "assume positive intent" or "listen to understand"—and reinforce these standards through consistent modeling and practice.

By prioritizing these best practices, leaders create opportunities for growth and understanding instead of division. Examples include:

- Facilitating open dialogue: Organize team sessions where differing perspectives are explored safely and constructively.
- Modeling civil discourse: Lead by example, approaching disagreements with curiosity and reframing conflict as a chance for mutual learning.
- Undertaking regular reflection: Incorporate opportunities for team feedback on communication norms to strengthen and adapt the approach over time.

When courageous leaders promote civil discourse as a core skill, they ensure that conflict becomes a pathway to understanding, trust, and innovation. Civil discourse strengthens a team's ability to navigate complex challenges, bridging differences and creating a foundation of psychological safety that endures beyond any single disagreement. It requires a sustained commitment to building a workplace culture where employees feel empowered to express themselves, listen actively, and find common ground amid polarization.

Courageous Leaders Can Act Now

As polarization increases, fueling uncertainty, courageous leaders like you are essential in transforming conflict into opportunities for collaboration and growth. The Agency Loop provides a powerful framework for navigating these challenges, helping leaders stay grounded in their core values while fostering a resilient workplace culture.

In the face of heightened polarization and societal shifts, courageous leaders lean into values like respect, integrity, transparency, and inclusivity. They model civil discourse by approaching disagreements with curiosity, asking questions to understand underlying perspectives rather than making assumptions. They create environments where differences are seen as strengths, not threats. By taking purposeful actions—such as setting clear behavioral expectations, providing training in active listening, and fostering psychological safety—leaders ensure that teams can engage openly and confidently, even amid external pressures.

Courageous leaders understand that growth is not a destination but an ongoing journey. They approach this journey as continuous learning, where building individuals' skills strengthens the team's collective ability to engage in civil discourse. By connecting civil discourse to shared values and purpose, and by creating spaces for reflection, experimentation, and learning, they empower their teams to embrace conflict as an integral part of the journey—one that leads to trust, resilience, and innovation.

As the workplace continues to evolve with technological advancements, shifting cultural dynamics, and heightened uncertainties, the need for courageous leadership grows even stronger. Your commitment to fostering inclusivity, respect, and civil discourse not only strengthens your team today but also lays the groundwork for a future where collaboration thrives amid diversity.

Make It Matter

Growth and courageous leadership don't happen by accident—they come from intentional choices, practiced over time. The following actions offer practical ways to apply what you've learned, whether through small shifts in daily behavior or larger commitments that influence your organization.

Start where you are. Even a 5 percent shift in how you show up can create meaningful change.

Small Actions
(5 Percent More Courageous—Start Today)

- Expand your perspective. Who in your workplace holds a different viewpoint from you? How can you reach out to build trust and understanding?
- Reflect on past conversations. Think about a recent discussion that became tense. What was your role in it, and how might you approach it differently next time?
- Model respect in everyday moments. What's one small way you can foster civil discourse in your daily interactions (e.g., listening fully before responding, assuming positive intent, or acknowledging different viewpoints)?

Medium Actions
(Influencing Your Immediate Sphere—within Weeks)

- Shape the culture around you. Where do you have influence over team dynamics or decisions? How can you foster respectful communication and reduce the impact of polarization?

- Set clear expectations for dialogue. What communication norms would help promote civil discourse on your team? How can you introduce or reinforce these in your workplace?
- Lead by example. Can you recall a moment when you successfully navigated a difficult conversation? How might sharing that experience help others learn and feel safe to engage in open dialogue?

Big Actions
(Shaping Systems and Culture—Ongoing Commitment)

- Take a proactive approach to polarization. How can you help your team or organization address divisive issues constructively? What conversations or initiatives need to happen?
- Equip your team with tools for better dialogue. What resources or training (like workshops on conflict resolution or active listening) could help your team develop stronger communication skills?
- Deescalate conflict with intention. How can you help your team engage in difficult conversations without escalating tension? What strategies or approaches would support a culture of open and respectful dialogue?

COURAGE FUELS
INNOVATION

CHAPTER 8

Courageous Leadership and the Rapid Rise of Innovation

Innovation has shaped incredible growth in our world, particularly since the Industrial Revolution, spanning how we communicate, interact, conduct business, travel, create, and grow. More recently, the idea of innovation has been tied to the development of technology and science, particularly on display during the COVID-19 era, when whole societies needed to adapt in order to overcome the reality of that moment.

Looking back to the Industrial Revolution, we see that technological innovation seems almost inevitable. Humanity's intense curiosity to explore what is possible has driven much of the advancement, particularly as access to new technologies like the internet, mobile phones, and the personal computer has spread access to information, computing power, and new ideas. We see the progress of innovation daily, from new drugs that begin to cure cancer and halt the AIDS epidemic, to the expansion of new clean energy sources, and efforts to finally reach viable desalination methods—potentially bringing clean, drinkable water to billions.

If innovation is happening all the time, then why is it something we need to explore in a book about leadership? Shouldn't we all just expect innovation to take place?

Just because it's expected doesn't mean we've figured out the human side of innovation. We call innovation a tension because it applies pressure to leaders to push the boundaries of what is possible. But that is never a smooth road, often asking leaders to face ever-changing obstacles and overcome new challenges. The pressure leaders face is different for each organization and team, so to better understand the pressure, let's look at some contributing factors.

Innovation is expensive, and in many cases, the stakes are high. Companies often have to sacrifice profit margins and dividends in service of future growth. During COVID-19, spending on innovation spiked as the world wrestled with the need to retool business models to meet a new normal, while also navigating supply chain shortages and competitive labor markets. The World Intellectual Property Organization (WIPO), the United Nations agency set up to serve the world's innovators and creators, released their annual Global Innovation Index report in 2024, where the number one finding showed that the spending of the COVID-19 era on innovation slowed dramatically in 2023. While companies continue investing in innovation (and will always do so), concerns about a potential recession in 2023 and 2024, coupled with rising interest rates, have made discretionary capital less available for use.[1]

Yet there is something curious about innovation. In 2018, PricewaterhouseCoopers (PwC) released a report claiming that, in general, there is no long-term correlation between the amount of money a company spends on its innovation efforts and its overall financial performance. So not only does investment not guarantee results, but companies are spending less now on innovation compared to when market conditions made it cheaper to borrow toward innovation. That's not to say that investors and key stakeholders don't expect a return on investment in innovation.[2]

One key bellwether of those returns is the pace of innovation, and while investment has gone down, acceleration of innovation continues. In the same WIPO Innovation report, the organization reports that their research supports Moore's law, which continues to hold, with a growth rate that supports the theory of doubling transistors on an integrated circuit every two years (though we may be getting closer to breaking the laws of physics if the law continues to hold).[3] The opening argument for the KPMG Global Tech Report 2024 shows that leaders and executives are struggling to keep up with the pace and are increasingly aware of their shortcomings in keeping up with innovation.[4] The pace of technological innovation continues to support renewed focus on innovation even if corporate leadership is struggling to keep up with that innovation.

Here's the big picture: innovation is an ongoing challenge—never fully solved and rarely easy to master—yet every organization must navigate it. This creates real tension for leaders, who are expected to drive innovation and guide their teams through its uncertainties. Technological advancements, in particular, amplify this challenge, with artificial intelligence (AI) emerging as one of the most disruptive innovations of our time. While AI promises efficiency and transformation, it also sparks anxiety, frustration, and even resistance. Courageous leadership requires addressing the underlying fear that comes with such rapid change. Today leaders are not only questioning AI's impact on their organizations but also grappling with the uncertainty it brings. However, while AI may dominate the current conversation, the more profound innovation lies in how we, as humans and leaders, evolve in response to change.

The world of artificial intelligence is one that we've been imagining and experimenting toward for a long time. From Asimov's *I, Robot*, to HAL 9000 in *2001: A Space Odyssey*, *The Terminator* and KITT from *Knight Rider* in the '80s, even to Data, an android struggling with its own humanity in *Star Trek: The Next Generation*. This is what we tend to do as humans—when it comes to innovation, if we can think of it, we begin to try to create it. These examples have helped fuel decades of research to bring us to our current moment.

AI, particularly generative AI and its offspring, represents tremendous opportunity as the next great leap in innovation. A leap that affects the whole world, similar to leaps like the advent of vaccines, television, cell phones, and the internet. All with ripple effects that could never have been known at the time. All of which pushed the boundaries of what is possible. And while those innovations seem familiar now—having been studied and analyzed ad nauseam—the lessons learned from them remain applicable to our current moment.

Now we are not experts in AI, so we aren't going to attempt to list all of the ways AI is changing the world. That list would be too exhaustive and likely out of date by the time you're reading this very sentence. But that's the point. AI represents the next frontier for great human advancement. As it is a frontier, we simply don't yet know where it will take humanity. But that doesn't mean we can't take lessons from how humans have handled innovation in the past. When we have approached great moments of innovation, like the introduction of the smartphone, there have often been advantages for those early adopters of the technology. Early movers in the market developed competitive advantages over those slow to adapt.

A classic example of failing to adapt quickly is BlackBerry and its demise due to the rise of smartphones like the iPhone. When the iPhone introduced a keyboardless design, BlackBerry remained confident that its keyboard-based model had a stronghold in the corporate market. However, as consumers embraced the iPhone's touch screen and the app ecosystem that transformed it into an all-in-one device, it became clear that a shift in consumer preferences was underway.

BlackBerry resisted this change, continuing to produce keyboard-based models long after touch-screen phones began to erode its market share. Over time, BlackBerry lost its competitive advantage, particularly in security, as other devices improved both their technology and operating systems. By the early 2010s, BlackBerry's market share plummeted from being the premier mobile gadget to less than 3 percent by 2013.[5] In 2016, the company pivoted, shifting its focus away from manufacturing mobile devices to concentrating on software and cybersecurity.[6]

We use this example because at one point, BlackBerry was the gold standard for mobile business communications. Their demise was very public, particularly because their market share dropped so quickly to less than 3 percent—a dramatic fall in the span of four years. This is a classic example of an organization that was unwilling or too slow to adapt, and it's a cautionary tale for innovation. It highlights the importance of early adoption and corporate agility. This story provides a stark reminder of the fear of being left behind, a fear that is especially relevant in the age of AI.

The Fear: No One Wants to Be Left Behind

In 2022, when generative AI made its debut, the narrative shifted. AI moved from being a tool focused on data synthesis through machine learning to something much more dynamic—an application capable of creation. Given the context of the post pandemic world, the timing couldn't have been more precarious. The thought of a workforce armed with tools that could multiply output or even replace employees at a fraction of the cost had corporate boards eagerly anticipating the potential. And from there, the pace of adoption exploded.

Fear of Missing Out

The rapid integration of AI into the workplace is where things differ from past technological frontiers. McKinsey's research noted that the organizational adoption of generative AI jumped from 33 percent in 2023 to 65 percent in 2024, marking a significant shift in just one year.[7] Similarly, KPMG's 2024 report on the pace of change revealed that many leaders are deeply concerned about missing out. They fear that if their organizations can't keep up with AI, they will fall behind.[8]

Fear of Being Unprepared

It's not just executives who feel this pressure. According to Mercer Global Talent Trends 2024, 60 percent of executives surveyed stated that the rapid pace of technological innovation—particularly AI—is outpacing their organizations' ability to reskill and redeploy their workforce.[9] Meanwhile, ADP's People at Work 2024 survey shows that employees who are most fearful of AI feel that their skills development is lagging behind AI's rapid evolution.[10] The impact of AI development, integration, and adaptation is undeniably central to the current workplace experience.

Fear of Underperforming

Yet while organizations and employees may feel like they are falling behind, AI represents a shift in innovation that's more egalitarian than previous technological advances due to its widespread accessibility. Unlike the advent of cell phones or the internet, access to both free and paid AI tools became available to billions of people over a short time between 2022 and 2023. What's more, AI's language processing models allow nearly anyone who uses the internet to engage with the technology, breaking down previous barriers that required specialized training to use new tools.

This broad access means that organizations, even those without a specific strategy or large capital, can begin experimenting with AI. While early access to the technology may have initially felt like a competitive advantage, many organizations that delayed or slowed their integration of AI will benefit from the maturation of AI products. The inherent learning nature of these products means that later adopters will be able to leverage improved systems, potentially leveling the playing field. *Harvard Business Review* research from 2024 shows that while the early pace of AI adoption might offer temporary competitive advantages, long-term success will depend more on proprietary data and organizational-specific resources paired with AI rather than just adopting AI itself.[11]

This dynamic ties back to the fears of underperformance and falling behind. There are many challenges associated with AI, such as fears of replacement, loss, and missing out. What makes innovation even more challenging is the dual role that leaders play in the process of implementing new tools like AI. They are required to keep pace with innovation and deliver continued expansion of results—all while knowing they are navigating uncharted territory, often with their teams' futures on the line.

Add to this the fact that leaders are humans too (shocking, we know)—with their own fears and pressures regarding their responsibilities. Moments of great innovation become much harder to balance and manage. It's a delicate task to drive change while navigating personal fears and uncertainties about the future.

Furthermore, while AI is a significant part of this moment, it's just that—a moment. We can't yet measure the full implications of AI or the full capabilities it represents. In this time, AI is simply a new tool, the next wave of innovation. And for leaders, while AI will change the way we work, it doesn't change the fundamental way humans have always navigated innovation.

The Answer: Courageous Leadership and Human Innovation

Throughout this chapter, we've discussed technological innovation, particularly AI, but what if the next great leap isn't about the tools we develop, but rather how we evolve as leaders and build teams that are equipped to thrive in times of change? In this sense, we're talking about human innovation. A wholesale redefinition of the roles and expectations we have in the workplace. A jump from the expectations of the command-and-control-style workplace of the Industrial Revolution, to the adaptive, responsive, and innovative workplace of the AI age. In this age of human innovation, leaders are going to play a pivotal role in two places: how they navigate change and how they enable their teams to capture and capitalize on their human capabilities.

Navigating Change

The responsibility of a courageous leader today is not just to adopt or lead innovation but to guide their teams through it. This is where courage and adaptability are paramount. Leaders are tasked with building the capacity within teams to change, transition, and develop the new skills needed to keep pace with ongoing innovation. Meanwhile leaders need to shield their organizations from external threats that might hinder their ability to navigate change. And while it's important for leaders to model the adoption of new technologies like AI, their true role lies in preparing their teams to embrace and capitalize on these changes, regardless of the challenges.

This moment in history is pivotal for leaders. In the past, it may have been possible to manage change haphazardly, but with the fast pace of innovation and the accessibility of new technologies, leaders must now lean into building the durable skill set required to navigate change effectively. And leaders can't rely solely on fear to motivate teams through change, using what John Kotter, well-known Harvard professor and thought leader on change, calls "the burning platform" method. Fear used to move teams off the burning platform only motivates teams to action, to survive the experience rather than to change through the experience.[12]

It takes courage to face this moment head-on. Leadership today is defined less by control and more by the ability to help teams thrive in an environment of constant innovation.

Enabling Human Capacity

The shift we're seeing is a fundamental change in how we view the value of individuals within organizations. It's no longer just about roles and titles, but about the broader skills and capabilities people bring to the table. With generative AI tools, individuals can now become productivity centers that rival whole teams. Generative AI has opened the door for a deeper understanding of human potential, allowing us to redefine how we assess, develop, and deploy skills in the workplace.

Historically, organizations have looked at roles and job descriptions to measure value. But in today's world, it's crucial to look beyond these formal definitions and understand the full range of human capabilities each team member offers. While this isn't a completely new approach, the tools we now have, especially through generative AI, allow us to assess and leverage these capabilities more effectively than ever before.

The introduction of AI, particularly large language models, marks a pivotal moment in how organizations align their understanding of human experience with their real-time needs. AI enables us to track and categorize capabilities in new ways, bridging gaps between what employees can do and what the organization needs.

As Josh Bersin notes in *Irresistible*, "We have moved from an economy where your employer defines your career to one where your experience, skills, and ambition drive success."[13] This shift isn't just about developing new capabilities; it's about organizations gaining the capacity to recognize and leverage those capabilities effectively.

Looking ahead, we see the skills required for the future of work are changing rapidly. By 2030, it's expected that 50 percent of the skills required today will be obsolete, with that number jumping to 68 percent when accounting for AI advancements.[14] With these projections in mind, leaders must not only understand the skills their teams possess today but actively plan for future skill development. This means investing in both new skills and those durable capabilities that will endure.

The bottom line? The future of work belongs to those who embrace adaptability. Leaders who take a proactive approach to mapping, developing, and sustaining critical durable skills will ensure that their teams remain resilient in the face of rapid transformation.

Embracing the Tension

Why does this represent tension for you as a leader? For most leaders, especially in more traditional, hierarchical structures, the experience has been one where success is measured by upward movement or staying within the same, defined roles. But as innovation disrupts the workplace, this outdated model of career progression becomes obsolete. Leaders will need to look beyond roles and titles, assessing talent based on the actual capabilities of individuals rather than their job descriptions.

The shift requires leaders to actively engage with their teams in new ways. They must assess talent based on real, tangible skills, offer opportunities for upskilling, and engage with team members on a more personal level to understand their growth potential and motivations. It's a significant shift in how we view leadership and how we view the value of the individual within the organization.

This is where courage becomes indispensable. Stepping into this new leadership age requires embracing the potential of human capabilities, not just managing team members according to traditional expectations. Leaders must take the leap into this new way of thinking to ensure their teams are equipped to succeed in an ever-evolving workplace.

Build Coaching Capacity as a Durable Skill

One of the best analogies for a courageous leader today is an athletics coach. Most of us have encountered a coach—whether in our own lives, in school, or through pop culture—who shaped our understanding of leadership. Of course, leading a team isn't a game. But that doesn't mean we can't draw valuable leadership lessons from coaching.

The idea of leadership as coaching isn't new. Carol Dweck[15] and Josh Bersin[16] talk about it in their books. Great coaches like Tony Dungy,[17] Phil Jackson,[18] and Pat Summitt[19] have all written about their approaches to leadership through coaching. We could go on and on. Coaching is especially relevant now because of the mindset coaches bring—one that prioritizes guidance over control. Our argument has always centered on leading with courage rather than fear. Yet as we've shared before, in times of uncertainty, teams look to leaders to provide stability amid chaos. Instead of defaulting to a command-and-control approach, effective leaders—like great coaches—find certainty not in rigid directives, but in how they navigate uncertainty with clarity, adaptability, and trust.

Coaching for Change

Coaches set team values and strategy, build a game plan, and prepare their teams—but they don't step onto the field. The players are the ones who execute, using their skills to win. Just like in the workplace, even the best-laid game plans often need to change in real time. A great coach communicates and realigns the team to those changes while empowering them to perform. Ultimately, while leaders may share some responsibilities with their teams, the bulk of the execution falls to team members—just as in sports, players are responsible for winning the game.

So what's the point? Courage isn't about eliminating pain or loss—it's about navigating the Moments That Matter. When uncertainty arises, fear takes hold—not just from not knowing what comes next, but sometimes from knowing exactly what's coming and the change it will bring.

Take AI as an example. We already know that change is happening, and it's accelerating. A leader's role isn't to control innovation itself, but to guide the human experience of change. As Brabandere notes in *The Forgotten Half of Change*, "The paradox is that while the world is changing faster than ever before, the human brain is the same old instrument it has been for hundreds, if not thousands, of years. That's too bad because the brain is the only tool that allows us to change our perceptions."[20] This is why navigating change isn't just about strategy—it's about leading people through the emotions that come with it.

Coaching to Enable Capacity

The human reaction to change is relatively constant. This is why coaching is a powerful model for courageous leadership. Great coaches model vulnerability, anchor their teams in shared values, view change as an opportunity, and create space for psychological safety. By doing so, they foster an environment where teams can adapt and innovate rather than retreat in fear.

In many cases, a coach doesn't know what talent they'll have at the start of a season. In the workplace, we have more control over recruitment, but even then, it's difficult to predict how new team members will develop. Good coaches fit people into their system;

the best coaches design the system around their people, leveraging strengths and mitigating weaknesses.

Our call to courage in the age of AI is about exploring possibilities. Leaders must rethink how they train, build, and retain skills—not just for today's needs, but for long-term adaptability. This isn't a new concept; generations of great leaders have focused on navigating change, fostering psychological safety, and managing conflict. But now, more than ever, we must commit to building these capabilities at all levels of our organizations.

Courageous leaders don't eliminate fear—they move through it, leaning on trust, curiosity, and resilience. As AI reshapes our world, the leaders who embrace these values will be the ones who guide their teams through uncertainty—unlocking potential rather than retreating into fear.

Courageous Leaders Act Now

Leaning into your values is critical during times of change. Remember, leaders are humans too. While you may experience fear in the face of rapidly evolving innovation, that fear can be a powerful tool. When you feel fear, it may also reflect the fears of your team members. This is where your ability to harness that experience becomes crucial—not just to empathize with your team but to create coaching opportunities that foster connection through shared experiences.

Change can be a time for reinvention. While you may not be able to control major organizational shifts—such as acquisitions, reorganizations, or layoffs—you can lay the foundation for your team's identity. Developing this new identity should center around a shared purpose, one that brings your team together. Cocreation can reinforce this process: you can shine as a coach, guiding your team as they come together to create that opportunity.

Even with the best plans in place, leaders can never fully predict how change will impact their teams. A plan gives you control over what you can, but you also need to prepare for setbacks, such as loss and failure. What defines leaders like you is your ability to align your actions with your values, turning setbacks into opportunities. Loss may come in the form of team identity changes or the departure of team members. Failure could arise during innovation or experimentation. However, if you help your team find meaning in these moments and respond with resilience, you can transform fear into an opportunity for growth, innovation, and navigating change.

Make It Matter

Growth and courageous leadership don't happen by accident—they come from intentional choices, practiced over time. The following actions offer practical ways to apply what you've learned, whether through small shifts in daily behavior or larger commitments that influence your organization.

Start where you are. Even a 5 percent shift in how you show up can create meaningful change.

Small Actions
(5 Percent More Courage—Start Today)

- Talk openly about change. Acknowledge that innovation brings uncertainty, and encourage team discussions to process it together.

- Ask thought-provoking questions. Shift the focus to possibilities by asking, "What's one way this change could help us work smarter?"
- Lead by example. Show your team that learning is a process by sharing how you're adapting and being honest about what you're still figuring out.

Medium Actions
(Influencing Your Immediate Sphere—within Weeks)

- Test small changes first. Try out new ideas or tools on a small scale before rolling them out fully. Gather feedback and adjust as needed.
- Create space for idea sharing. Hold team discussions where employees can share their thoughts on upcoming changes and suggest solutions.
- Encourage team connections. Pair employees with colleagues from different teams who have successfully navigated similar changes to share insights.

Big Actions
(Shaping Systems and Culture—Ongoing Commitment)

- Recognize adaptability in performance reviews. Highlight employees who embrace change and contribute to innovative solutions.
- Make learning easy to access. Build a shared space for documenting best practices, lessons learned, and useful resources.

- Break down silos. Strengthen collaboration across departments so diverse perspectives help shape new ideas and long-term strategies.

COURAGE
IS HOPE

CHAPTER 9

The Future We Choose

The future is not something that simply happens to us. It is something we create. And in this moment—right now—we are making a choice.

With all this uncertainty and change comes an opportunity to redefine how we work, live, and lead. The rapid advancement of technology, shifts in global demographics, and evolving societal values give us a once-in-a-generation chance to shape the future in ways that foster inclusion, creativity, and purpose. This is a moment for courage—to build a world where people feel empowered to be authentic, find meaning in their work, and contribute to something larger than themselves.

Fear will always be present. It will whisper that the safest option is to maintain control, to resist change, to retreat into what is comfortable. But courageous leadership isn't about eliminating fear. It's about walking through it, grounded in our values. It's about making intentional decisions, not just reacting to the pressures around us.

That is what The Agency Loop is all about. It is a tool, not a rigid formula. A practice, not a prescription. Leadership is a series of choices—daily, intentional, values-driven. The leaders who will shape the future are not those who wait for clarity, but those who move forward despite uncertainty.

We are standing at a threshold. We can allow fear and polarization to dictate the future, or we can choose a different path—one that embraces innovation, equity, and the potential of AI to enhance, rather than replace, human leadership. The allure of strongmen—whether in politics or the workplace—is real. They offer certainty in uncertain times, control in moments of chaos. But history has shown us time and again that their leadership is a dead end. Control stifles creativity. Division erodes trust. Fear crushes potential.

True leadership does not come from domination, but from courage. From the willingness to embrace complexity rather than simplify it. From the strength to empower others, rather than hoard power for oneself.

But courage doesn't have to be loud or dramatic. It doesn't require a main stage or a perfect plan. The future isn't shaped in one bold act—it is built through small, daily acts of courage. A conversation that challenges the status quo. A decision to stay curious instead of defensive. A willingness to embrace the discomfort of growth. These small shifts—the 5 percent shifts—may seem insignificant in the moment, but over time, they are what create lasting change.

This is why *Star Trek* has always been more than just a vision of the future. It represents what is possible when we commit to curiosity over fear, to collaboration over control, to purpose over power. It is a future where leaders do not let uncertainty paralyze them but instead see it as a frontier—one that must be explored with courage.

And that is the future we choose.

Not because it is easy. Not because the path is clear. But because we believe in what is possible. Because we have hope. Hope, that through courage, we can build a world where trust replaces fear, where innovation is driven by inclusion, and where leadership is not about control, but about possibility.

The call to courage has been made. The future is being written.

And someday, we hope you'll look back on this moment, on the choices you made, and instead of asking, "What just happened?"— you'll know.

You'll know that you helped build something better.

You'll know that you chose courage over fear.

Additional Resources for Your Courageous Leadership Journey

As you continue your journey toward courageous leadership, it's essential to have the right tools and support to reinforce your growth. This section provides additional resources designed to help you apply the concepts and practices discussed throughout the book. These resources will support you in navigating the challenges and uncertainties you'll face as a leader, equipping you with practical tools, further reading, and exercises to deepen your leadership practice. The journey of courageous leadership is ongoing, and these resources are here to help you continue evolving with intention.

In Appendix 1, we introduce Taylor and Justin, two composite leaders whose stories reflect the challenges many leaders face today. Through their experiences, we'll explore how the forces shaping today's workplace impact leadership in different ways. Their journeys serve as case studies, showing how The Agency Loop provides a practical, values-driven approach to making tough decisions, confronting tension, and turning uncertainty into opportunity. By following Taylor's and Justin's paths, you'll gain valuable insights to help you lead with intention, even when faced with uncertainty.

In Appendix 2, you'll find resources focused on The Agency Loop. These include exercises designed to deepen your practice of authenticity and agency, guiding you through moments of tension and dissonance. These tools will help you reflect, learn, and take intentional action toward growth.

As you explore these resources, remember that they are part of your ongoing leadership development. The tools and insights here complement the core concepts in this book, but your journey doesn't stop here. Keep these tools in mind as you continue to evolve as a courageous leader, navigating the complexities of your role with intention and confidence.

Appendix 1: The Case Studies

Introducing Taylor and Justin, Leaders Just Like You

Leadership today is a high-stakes endeavor, shaped by unrelenting fear and uncertainty. To give you a clear and cohesive leadership story from start to finish, we wanted a narrative thread that would tie it all together. To ensure no real-life careers were harmed in the writing of this book, allow us to introduce our entirely fictional, totally "not-based-on-any-true-story-or-person" friends, Taylor and Justin.

These composite characters are thoughtfully crafted from the collective experiences, challenges, and successes of countless individuals in today's workplaces. They embody the duality of modern leadership: the internal and external struggles that arise when fear takes root in the face of uncertainty. They serve as proxies for the countless leaders grappling with the pressures of deprioritization of DEI, technological disruption, political and social polarization, and other forces reshaping our workplaces and society.

Through Taylor and Justin, we'll explore how fear—whether driven by external pressures or internal insecurities—shapes decision-making, influences leadership behaviors, and impacts team dynamics. Their journeys reflect the realities of leading in an environment where unpredictability is the norm and where leadership choices carry profound consequences.

In the case studies ahead, you'll follow Taylor and Justin as they navigate three of the most pressing uncertainties facing leaders today: deprioritization of DEI, political and social polarization, and the rapid rise of innovation. Each case study will illustrate how these forces shape their decisions and the ripple effects on their teams and organizations.

We hope you'll see your own challenges reflected in their stories and draw inspiration from their courage. Like Taylor and Justin, you face moments of tension and transformation that demand courage, trust, and resilience. Their experiences will reveal how courageous leadership can break the cycle of fear and transform challenges into opportunities for growth, trust, and innovation.

Taylor and Justin's Moment That Mattered: What Just Happened?

It was an early Tuesday morning, and the air in the conference room felt heavy. Taylor, a senior manager on the digital transformation team, shifted uncomfortably in her seat along the wall, scanning the faces of her colleagues as they trickled in, trying to ignore the tightness in her chest. The CEO had scheduled an unexpected all-hands meeting, and the usual buzz of excitement that often accompanied these announcements was absent. A staff-only calendar invite from her manager followed the announcement.

Taylor knew something was up. She had been here before. When the chief digital officer scheduled unplanned staff meetings, it meant something was changing. She wondered, *Now what?*

Over the years, she had watched as more and more leaders emulated the CEO—loud, arrogant, dismissive. The CEO's leadership mantra was clear: control everything and deliver results at any cost. He bulldozed through obstacles, through people, with very little regard for the impact. And it worked—at least, that's what the promotions and recognition awards seemed to suggest. The company was now led by clones of him, and they set the tone for the entire culture.

The recent acquisition of a specialized AI firm in Nashville was already creating friction. Taylor wondered if this was what the meeting was about. The Nashville team, known for its collaborative and values-driven approach, felt like an odd fit in a company dominated by results-at-any-cost leadership. Their expertise in ethical AI and inclusivity clashed with the San Francisco team's relentless focus on speed and scale. She couldn't help but wonder how long it would take before the Nashville team's culture was bulldozed—or if they would manage to push back against the company's top-down, authoritarian style.

Across the room, Justin, the senior manager of global integrations, leaned back in his chair, casually checking his phone. He, too, had been here before. Unlike Taylor, he welcomed the uncertainty. He admired the CEO and the leaders who had risen to power. They were decisive, unflinching, always delivering results. To Justin, that's what great leadership looked like. Today was just another chance to prove himself.

The chief digital officer took her seat at the head of the table, flanked by her leadership team. Without wasting any time, she launched into the announcement.

"We're introducing a new enterprise AI system," the CDO began. "This will fundamentally change how we work. By using AI to increase the collective intelligence of the entire organization, we'll move faster than ever. This system was developed by our newly acquired team in Nashville, who bring invaluable expertise. Our organization will lead the integration and implementation of this system. The CEO expects full adoption across the company within thirty days. No exceptions."

The room fell silent. No one dared to ask questions—this wasn't the place for that.

Taylor's heart sank. *Mandatory. No exceptions.* She'd seen it coming. This was the fourth major implementation her team was involved in this year without a break. The relentless speed and pressure were suffocating. She could already see the exhaustion in her team's faces, the unspoken worry about how they'd survive another impossible deadline. Yet the bigger fear gnawed at her: What would happen if she pushed back? She knew the answer. This company didn't reward hesitation. Raising concerns wasn't just unwelcome—it was risky. Machines over people. Efficiency over humanity. Control over collaboration. And fear—fear of being seen as weak—was what kept it all in place.

Justin's heart raced for different reasons. *Finally!* AI was the future, and he was ready to lead the way. The acquisition of the Nashville team brought exciting new technology to the company, but their emphasis on ethical AI and inclusivity felt like roadblocks to progress. *We don't have time for that*, he thought. *This is about results, not ideals.* He saw them as talented but impractical—a group that would have to adapt to the company's faster, more aggressive culture. This was the kind of challenge he thrived on. His confidence came not from introspection, but from blind faith in his ability to deliver results at any cost. Maybe this would be his chance to catch the CEO's attention. He was ready to prove that he was cut from the same cloth.

Taylor Experiences Dissonance

Back at her desk, Taylor stared at her computer screen, trying to focus on catching up on email. But her gaze softened, and her head fell heavily into her hands. Her team was already struggling to keep up with their current workload. Now with the pressure of AI looming, she knew they were looking to her for guidance. But how could she lead them through this implementation when she herself had questions about the impact of the technology and felt like this latest whiplash in priorities could be the last straw for some of her team members?

When she met with her team later that day, the tension was thick in the room. They had questions, real concerns about the AI implementation schedule and what the tech meant for their jobs and their futures. Taylor could see the fear in their eyes, and it mirrored her own. This was her moment—she knew exactly what needed to be said. But another feeling rose up, tightening in her chest: fear. Not of the work, not of the AI rollout, but of what speaking up would mean. What if pushing back made her a target? What if she lost credibility? She had seen what happened to leaders who questioned the status quo. Her courage flickered, then faded. Silence was safer. The company's culture didn't leave room for that kind of discussion.

"Let's just focus on getting through this," she said, deflecting their deeper concerns. Her words felt hollow, and her team knew it.

The team left the meeting more uncertain than before, and Taylor's heart sank. She felt like she was failing them. Each day, she had the opportunity to lead with empathy, but the courage to act was overshadowed by the risk of being seen as weak in this fast-paced, results-driven culture.

Meanwhile, Taylor's silence was weighing heavily on her team. One afternoon, one of her most trusted team members asked for a one-on-one meeting.

"We need you to lead us," he said bluntly. "You've been quiet, and we feel lost."

His words cut deep. That evening, Taylor sat in her office and asked herself, *What happened today? Why do I feel so gutted by what my team member said to me?* She took a moment to get curious about what she was feeling. Taylor realized that her fear of appearing weak had caused her to withdraw when her team needed her the most. She had been so focused on not making waves in the company's culture that she had abandoned her natural leadership instincts— empathy and compassion.

She dug a little deeper. She had been successful in the company so far. Always delivering results for her leadership. What was it this time that gave her pause? She had no clue what was going to happen with this new tool they were integrating. She realized that she had no experience using generative AI, and that everything in the news told her she was already behind learning about it. It was weakness in not looking like she knew what she was doing that kept her silent, and she began to see that leading with silence wasn't leadership at all. She had let the fear of appearing weak steal her courage, but it was time to reclaim it and lead with compassion.

Taylor made a decision: she wasn't going to let fear dictate her leadership any longer. The weight of silence had cost her team's trust, and she refused to make that mistake again. She didn't have all the answers, but she didn't need to—not if she led with honesty, empathy, and action. Tomorrow, she would start the conversation, not with certainty, but with the courage to listen, learn, and lead differently.

Justin Experiences Dissonance

In the weeks that followed, the pressure to meet the thirty-day adoption deadline intensified. Justin's team worked around the clock, prioritizing speed and efficiency over collaboration or inclusivity. His interactions with the Nashville team were curt and transactional.

Then, during a cross-functional meeting with key stakeholders, a Nashville engineer raised a concern. "We need to address gaps in our testing data," she said. "The current model excludes key user groups. If we roll this out as-is, it could lead to serious usability issues."

Justin barely looked up. "We can refine it after launch," he replied. "Right now, we need to deliver." To him, her approach was just another example of the Nashville team's slower, more idealistic style—a style that didn't align with the company's culture or priorities. *They'll need to get used to how we do things*, he thought dismissively.

The engineer didn't back down. She presented examples of how these gaps had led to AI failures in other organizations, costing millions in revenue and reputational damage. She added, "Addressing this now will strengthen the rollout and position us for long-term success."

The room fell silent. For a moment, Justin felt his confidence waver. Could this issue actually impact the results he was so focused on delivering? He brushed it aside, doubling down on his mandate to meet the deadline. "We're moving on."

Weeks later, the rollout went live, but cracks began to show almost immediately:

- Key clients reported usability issues, particularly among underrepresented groups.
- Feedback from internal teams revealed frustration over the system's limitations, undermining trust and morale.

The CEO called an emergency meeting, and Justin walked in, expecting a tough discussion. Instead, he faced a storm.

"You were put in charge to lead. How could you let this happen?" the CEO yelled. "You failed. Your team doesn't know what they are doing, and now look where we are. Fix it. Or don't expect to stick around."

Justin felt the words hit like a punch to the gut. Everything he had believed about leadership—about control, decisiveness, and speed—crumbled in an instant. He had spent years telling himself he was fearless, that his unwavering confidence made him a strong leader. But now, sitting under the weight of failure, he saw it clearly: *he had been leading from fear all along.* Fear of losing status. Fear of questioning the CEO's approach. Fear of looking weak. And that fear had driven every choice he made. Now he was on the verge of being discarded.

That night, Justin sat in his office replaying the day's events in his mind. He couldn't shake the Nashville engineer's words—or the data she had presented about the rollout failure. "She was right," he admitted. "I ignored her. I wanted everyone to know I was the leader and I had things under control. But she was trying to make this better. I didn't listen."

It wasn't just the failure that stung—it was realizing that

his leadership style, built on emulating the CEO's authoritarian approach, had created the conditions for that failure. He had dismissed the Nashville team's expertise, overlooked the value of inclusivity, and prioritized speed over quality.

For the first time, Justin saw the Nashville team's approach—emphasizing inclusivity and collaboration—not as naive, but as essential. Their culture wasn't the problem. *Maybe it's ours that needs to change*, he thought. He realized that fostering collaboration and integrating diverse perspectives wasn't just a "nice-to-have"—it was a business necessity.

Justin made a decision: he needed to rebuild trust, not just with his team but with the Nashville group he had dismissed. And to do that, he would have to embrace a new way of leading—one that prioritized listening, learning, and aligning his actions with the values he had long ignored.

Taylor and Justin Run the Loop

Taylor and Justin both faced the same win-at-all-costs culture that is, unfortunately, and increasingly, present in tech companies, but their responses were different. Taylor felt the tension from within—her silence in the face of pressure, her fear of leading with empathy. Justin experienced tension stemming from his overconfidence, rooted in blind faith in authoritarian leadership, and his dismissal of inclusivity as a vital component of success. But in the end, both learned that true leadership isn't about control—it's about courage. Not only the courage to take different actions, but the courage to take a hard look in the mirror at themselves. It is the introspective look in the mirror that drops them into the authenticity phase of The Agency Loop.

Authenticity Phase

When Taylor stopped and got curious about the moment she experienced, she realized that she was leading in a fear-based culture where leaders prioritized control over empathy. She feared that a mandatory AI adoption would hurt her team's morale, and she wanted to lead with authenticity and inclusion but struggled within the company's fast-paced, results-driven environment. Taylor hesitated to voice her concerns about the unrealistic AI implementation timeline, fearing she would be labeled as negative or resistant to change. Her values were in conflict with her environment, and this experience brought to life that dissonance in a way she had never felt before.

Justin stopped and began to confront the fallout from the failed rollout and the CEO's public humiliation. He had dismissed the Nashville team's concerns about inclusivity, prioritizing speed and control to prove himself in a fear-based, authoritarian culture. Emulating the CEO's style had seemed like the path to success, but the failure exposed its flaws—eroding trust within his team and undermining the very results he had been chasing. The dissonance he felt forced him to get clear on what values he actually held close, rather than continuing down a path of blind emulation. For the first time, he started to recognize that inclusivity and collaboration weren't distractions but could be essential for long-term success, sparking the beginning of a shift in his leadership approach.

When they both got curious about themselves and their actions, they began to better understand where the dissonance was coming from and what to do with the resulting tension.

Let's take a look at how they walked through the authenticity phase of the loop.

Leadership Takeaways

Courageous leadership, particularly in the authenticity phase, is built on a foundation of vulnerability and self-compassion. Both Justin and Taylor demonstrated that by confronting their imperfections and realigning their leadership with their values, they were able to foster trust, resilience, and growth within themselves and their teams.

For Justin, embracing vulnerability meant acknowledging his missteps and recognizing that his failure to value diverse perspectives had eroded trust and hindered collaboration. By shifting his definition of excellence from control and speed to inclusivity and trust, he began to lay the groundwork for a more resilient and effective team.

Taylor showed self-compassion in recognizing that her fear of being labeled resistant had kept her silent, and she took intentional steps to address her mistakes. By being transparent about her concerns and modeling resilience in the face of uncertainty, she demonstrated the power of growth through reflection and action.

Vulnerability allows leaders to connect authentically with others, fostering an environment where teams feel safe to share ideas, voice concerns, and take risks. Self-compassion provides the emotional grounding leaders need to acknowledge their imperfections and grow from them without succumbing to guilt or shame.

When leaders are honest about their mistakes and demonstrate a willingness to adapt, they create environments of openness, trust, and curiosity—where both leaders and teams can thrive. Having walked through this phase of authenticity, Justin and Taylor are now better prepared to think about and plan their next decisive moves with their teams, armed with clarity, courage, and a renewed commitment to their values.

Moving into the Agency Phase

Both leaders came to understand that the gaps between their values and environment were real, and closing them was important to them. They also recognized that knowledge wasn't enough. Each felt compelled to take action to close the gap. For real, lasting change, both would need to take bold, decisive action—focusing on what was within their control. This was their opportunity to exercise their agency. They still asked questions as part of the process, but this time the questions were meant to align their action with their values better and get clear about what those actions meant.

Let's take a look at how they walked through the agency phase of the loop.

Leadership Takeaway

Acting with intention and decisiveness means recognizing what's within your control and taking bold, values-aligned actions to bridge the gap between where you are and where you aspire to be. For Taylor, this involved stepping out of her comfort zone to challenge her silence, act on her curiosity, and empower her team in alignment with her values of empathy and inclusion. She recognized that fostering an inclusive environment required intentional action, even in a fear-driven culture.

For Justin, this phase required breaking free from the fear-based patterns he had emulated. By seeking help, prioritizing collaboration, and addressing the gaps in his team's knowledge and skills, he began to redefine leadership as a shared effort rather than a solitary pursuit. He learned that vulnerability and collaboration are not signs of weakness but sources of strength that build trust and drive innovation.

Decisiveness isn't about perfection or control; it's about taking calculated risks, asking the right questions, and aligning actions with values. Both leaders demonstrated that courage in leadership is not about knowing all the answers but about creating the conditions for curiosity, trust, and adaptability to flourish. By doing so, they began to transform their teams into resilient, collaborative units capable of thriving in uncertainty and change.

Growth Phase

The actions both leaders took in the agency phase set them on transformative paths as leaders. For Taylor, the path was one of finding the courage to move beyond the paralysis of fear, embracing empathy and inclusion as her guiding principles. For Justin, the journey was liberating—he let go of the burden of control and began to embrace collaboration and shared responsibility. While his fear of failure still lingered, he found courage in knowing that leadership doesn't require having all the answers but rather creating the conditions for others to succeed. Both leaders came to recognize that growth is an ongoing process, and a leader's journey is never static. To continue evolving, they would need to reflect, adapt, and learn from their experiences.

Let's take a look at how they walked through the growth phase of the loop.

Leadership Takeaway

Adaptability and growth as a leader require more than just reacting to external challenges—they demand intentional reflection, personal evolution, and a commitment to continuous learning. For Taylor, growth meant recognizing the unintended consequences of her actions and adapting her approach to better support her team. By fostering resilience and creating mechanisms for feedback, she cultivated a culture of trust, curiosity, and shared accountability.

For Justin, growth was about stepping beyond the limits of his old leadership style and embracing the power of collaboration. By seeking and valuing feedback, he identified areas for improvement and began experimenting with new approaches to empower his team. Through small, intentional changes, he built a foundation of trust and innovation that aligned with his evolving values.

True growth happens when leaders are willing to reflect on their actions, adapt to the needs of their teams, and prioritize learning over perfection. Leaders who embrace curiosity and vulnerability create environments where they and their teams can navigate setbacks, find new opportunities, and thrive in a culture of shared growth.

Closing the Loop

Taylor and Justin have completed their first cycle of The Agency Loop—moving through authenticity, agency, and growth. They've learned valuable lessons and faced challenges that shaped their leadership. Let's see what they learned.

Taylor Closes the Loop

Taylor's journey through The Agency Loop demonstrates that courageous leadership is an ongoing cycle of reflection, action, and learning. By confronting her fears, aligning her decisions with her values, and embracing vulnerability, Taylor strengthened trust, curiosity, and resilience within her team. Her intentional efforts to create an inclusive environment illustrate the transformative power of courageous leadership. Each loop she completes prepares her to meet new challenges with confidence and clarity, proving that authentic leadership grows stronger over time.

Justin Closes the Loop

Justin's progression through The Agency Loop highlights the power of transformation. Moving from a rigid, authoritarian style to a more collaborative, values-driven approach, he embraced curiosity, feedback, and empathy as essential elements of leadership. His willingness to adapt not only improved his team's cohesion and performance but set an example for others in the organization. Justin's journey reinforces that courageous leadership is about evolving through self-awareness, vulnerability, and intentional action, creating environments where trust, resilience, and inclusivity thrive.

Closing This Loop and Running Another

As leadership evolves, so do the challenges. New team dynamics, changing organizational priorities, and external pressures will always arise, but these don't stop the cycle—they become the foundation for the next.

By committing to this ongoing loop, Taylor, Justin, and any courageous leader build resilience, adaptability, and deeper insight. Every cycle of The Agency Loop strengthens their ability to lead with authenticity, courage, and clarity. As they step into the next cycle, they carry the lessons learned with them, embracing the challenges ahead with a greater sense of purpose and leadership.

Leadership isn't a destination—it's a practice. And with each new cycle, there's more opportunity to grow, to inspire, and to lead with even greater impact.

Make It Matter

Now that you've seen Taylor and Justin navigate through The Agency Loop, it's time to reflect on how their journey applies to your own leadership. What key takeaways can you identify from their process that you can integrate into your leadership approach?

- Takeaway: What insights did you gain from watching Taylor and Justin move through the loop? How do you see the loop playing out in your own leadership—what phases might you revisit or enter next?
- Reflect: What moments in your leadership have brought you face-to-face with dissonance, fear, or uncertainty? How did you respond, and what did you learn from those responses?
- Apply: How can you lean into your core values, like Taylor and Justin did, to guide your actions when faced with tough decisions or moments of change in your organization?
- Act: What's one small, intentional step you can take today to start your own cycle of growth? It might be as simple as asking yourself a challenging question, seeking feedback from your team, or taking a moment to listen more deeply.

Leadership is an ongoing cycle of reflection, action, and growth. What's the next step in your loop?

Case Study #1:
Addressing the Deprioritization of DEI

We return to Justin at a pivotal moment—another opportunity for him to run The Agency Loop, this time in the face of his company's quiet deprioritization of diversity, equity, and inclusion. As he navigates the pressure to deliver results in a shifting culture, his leadership choices will shape his team's performance and their trust in him.

As you read, put yourself in the mindset of a member of his team. What's working? What's not? Where does he step up, and where does he fall short? Most importantly, what would you need from him as a leader?

The company's acquisition of a specialized AI firm in Nashville signals a strategic pivot, but it also reflects a quiet deprioritization of its public commitment to diversity, equity, and inclusion. While the move is framed as a way to enhance technological capabilities and streamline operations, it sidelines previously stated DEI goals in favor of rapid integration and cost management. This decision sends ripples through the San Francisco office, raising questions about the company's evolving values and priorities.

This shift occurs against the backdrop of a changing political and cultural climate, where DEI initiatives are increasingly seen as expendable. While the company had previously championed inclusivity, these efforts are now viewed as obstacles to speed and meritocracy, creating unease among employees and leaders alike. For senior leaders like Justin, the strain is palpable. The CEO's message is unrelenting: results matter above all else. Under intense pressure to perform, senior managers are given little room to question directives or voice concerns—only to execute. This top-down culture prioritizes rapid delivery over inclusivity or long-term strategy, forcing leaders to make difficult trade-offs.

As the leader of the process integration team, Justin is tasked with ensuring a smooth integration of AI systems into existing workflows. This involves navigating the cultural tensions between the fast-paced, results-driven environment of San Francisco and the more collaborative style he observes in the Nashville team. Until now, Justin has quietly accepted the company's deprioritization of DEI, rationalizing it as an unfortunate but necessary cost of doing business. His primary focus on delivering outcomes has often come at the expense of fostering inclusivity or questioning the cultural implications of these shifts.

Recognizing Dissonance: Trigger a New Loop

Justin's trigger moment comes during a cross-functional meeting, where a junior engineer from the Nashville office—a first-generation immigrant—questions why inclusivity seems to be taking a back seat in the company's new initiatives. The engineer highlights how the lack of diverse perspectives in AI testing could limit the system's broader applicability and alienate key user groups. Initially, Justin deflects the critique, focused on meeting tight deadlines. But when the engineer presents a compelling example—how inclusivity in design directly drives market expansion—Justin pauses.

This is the first time Justin connects inclusivity with measurable business outcomes. Until now, he had seen inclusivity as a "soft" concern, unrelated to the hard metrics of success that dominate his daily priorities. But hearing how the lack of diverse perspectives could limit the very innovation the company needs to thrive forces Justin to reevaluate. The realization isn't just uncomfortable—it's activating.

This moment of recognition serves as Justin's trigger, setting off The Agency Loop. He begins to reflect on how his actions—and inactions—align with his values and starts to identify intentional steps he can take to bridge the gap between his beliefs and the environment he operates in.

Fueled by this moment of clarity, Justin takes deliberate steps to foster empathy and understanding within his team. He begins by acknowledging differences openly, encouraging team members to share their perspectives in structured and respectful ways. While uncomfortable at first, these conversations reveal insights that strengthen cohesion and collaboration. Justin also advocates for reinvesting in inclusivity initiatives, presenting his case not as a moral argument, but as a strategic necessity for driving innovation and maintaining a competitive edge.

As the work continues, Justin recognizes that his ability to navigate these tensions is critical—not just for his team's success, but for the company's survival in a fast-changing market. His journey reflects the power of The Agency Loop, where intentional reflection and action transform dissonance into a pathway for growth and courageous leadership.

Get Curious: What Just Happened?

Before we dive into the next phase of Justin's journey, let's get curious. Imagine you are on Justin's team, sitting in that cross-functional meeting when the junior engineer raises concerns about inclusivity. You watch Justin's initial reaction—focused on the deadline—but then see him pause, reconsider, and shift his perspective.

- Does Justin's reaction to the engineer's question make you feel more confident in his leadership or more uncertain?

- How could Justin support you while making space for other concerns and still driving results?
- If you were Justin, what would you have done differently?

Justin's journey reflects the evolving dynamics of organizational priorities and the quiet deprioritization of diversity, equity, and inclusion. His recent recognition of DEI's importance for driving innovation and business outcomes is coupled with a deeper realization: how he shows up as a leader profoundly impacts team culture. Justin begins to see that his previous authoritarian, results-driven approach has unintentionally stifled inclusivity and collaboration. This awareness challenges him to reevaluate his leadership style and adopt practices that build trust, cohesion, and a thriving, inclusive environment.

As organizations face growing external pressures and shifting internal priorities, employees and leaders alike grapple with the implications of deprioritizing DEI. For many, this retreat evokes fears of losing belonging, trust, and the values that once guided the company's vision. Leaders, too, may struggle with reconciling business demands with the long-term risks of sidelining inclusivity, creating further uncertainty. Courageous leaders, however, recognize that fostering inclusion and trust is not a distraction but a strategic necessity for innovation and resilience. By creating spaces for open dialogue and valuing diverse perspectives, they help teams navigate these tensions and build unity amid challenging times.

Using The Agency Loop to Overcome the Deprioritization of DEI

Leaders can leverage The Agency Loop to foster psychological safety as they navigate the challenges of the reprioritization of DEI. By intentionally creating spaces where team members feel heard and valued, leaders can counteract the negative effects of withdrawing from DEI, transforming fear and resistance into opportunities for growth and collaboration.

To illustrate this approach, we'll lean on Justin's examples, demonstrating how courageous leaders cultivate psychological safety in times of uncertainty by leaning into their values, controlling what they can, and finding meaning through experimentation.

When we first met Justin in this chapter, he was navigating the high-pressure integration of a new team amid a culture retreating from DEI commitments. His journey forced him to confront his assumptions about leadership and the role of inclusivity in achieving results. Earlier, we asked you to step into Justin's shoes and consider how you might approach his challenges. Now it is time to see what he did.

Start with Authenticity

Justin begins by openly acknowledging the cultural differences between the San Francisco and Nashville teams, as well as the uncertainties that accompany the acquisition. By sharing his own concerns and inviting his team to do the same, Justin demonstrates integrity and creates an environment where transparency is valued.

He models empathy by actively listening to his team's perspectives and fostering an inclusive dialogue, ensuring everyone feels heard. This approach helps bridge the gap between differing work styles and sets a foundation for psychological safety within the team.

Exercise Agency

Justin exercises his agency to foster psychological safety on his team by addressing tensions and fostering inclusivity during a period of significant organizational change. Despite the company's results-driven, top-down culture, he acknowledges the operational and cultural differences between the San Francisco and Nashville teams, fostering respect for diverse perspectives.

Justin creates structured opportunities for his team to voice their opinions, even when they differ from his own, demonstrating that all input is valued. By modeling collaboration and prioritizing empathy, he reinforces trust and cohesion within his team, showing that inclusivity is not just a value but a necessity for navigating uncertainty and achieving long-term success.

Embrace Growth

Justin demonstrates embracing growth by adapting to the challenges and opportunities presented during the company's organizational changes. Recognizing the cultural differences between the fast-paced San Francisco team and the more collaborative Nashville team, he adjusts his leadership style to bridge these gaps, leveraging the strengths of both groups.

Justin fosters a growth mindset within his team, framing the integration of AI and the uncertainties of change as opportunities to learn and innovate. He invests in developing his own understanding of AI systems and ensures his team has access to training, equipping them to handle the transition effectively.

Additionally, Justin seeks feedback from team members to better understand their needs and concerns, modeling humility and a commitment to continuous improvement. By approaching challenges with curiosity and adaptability, Justin creates an environment where his team feels empowered to grow and succeed—even as the company retreats from its DEI commitments. His intentional actions ensure that inclusivity and psychological safety remain a priority, despite broader organizational changes.

Make It Matter

Now imagine you're sitting in a meeting led by Justin. He just made a big decision, and the team is reacting. As you head to grab a coffee with a teammate, the conversation turns to what just happened. You're trying to make sense of it. Was this the right call? How does it affect you?

- What's your gut reaction to how Justin is leading? How does his approach make you feel as a member of his team?
- What do you think he did well? Where do you think he could have handled things differently?
- How do you think his leadership is impacting psychological safety on the team? Are people feeling safe to express themselves?
- If you were in his shoes, what would you have done differently? What kind of leader would you want to be in this situation?

Justin's story highlights the challenges of leading inclusively and creating psychological safety when DEI is being deprioritized. His choices weren't perfect, but he used The Agency Loop to take intentional steps to create a more inclusive environment.

Now take a moment to think about your own workplace.

Where do you see similar challenges? What opportunities do you have to lead with courage?

Use these questions to explore what this means for you:

- What stood out to you most about how Justin handled this situation? Why?
- Have you seen similar challenges in your own workplace? How did they play out?
- What's one way you could apply these insights in your leadership?
- What's one step—big or small—you can take this week to foster a more inclusive workplace?

Case Study #2:
Addressing Political and Social Polarization

Let's return to Justin at another critical juncture—this time navigating the rising tensions of polarization within his team and the broader organization. As external pressures seep into workplace dynamics, he faces a new challenge: maintaining collaboration and trust in an increasingly divided environment.

Once again, Justin has an opportunity to run The Agency Loop. His leadership choices will determine whether his team fractures under opposing viewpoints or finds a way to move forward together.

As you read, put yourself on his team. How does he handle the tension? Where does he create space for discourse, and where does he miss the mark? Most importantly, how would you want him to lead at this moment?

A merging of two company cultures, the public deprioritization of DEI, and the impact of a contentious election create a simmering tension that is beginning to boil over. What starts as minor differences in communication and working styles escalates into full-blown social and political conflicts within teams, and senior leaders like Justin find themselves caught in the middle of it all. In an environment where collaboration is key to driving innovation, these conflicts pose a serious threat to the company's ability to move forward.

Justin is grappling with significant divisions within his team. Two of his team members find themselves on opposite sides of a political spectrum that increasingly influences workplace conversations. One is vocal about her conservative views, while the other leans toward progressive values, affecting the team's ability to collaborate effectively. Justin, whose political views align more closely with one of the team members, feels the pressure to do something or face the risk of his team imploding under the tension.

Recognizing Dissonance:
Trigger The Agency Loop

During a team meeting, a heated argument breaks out between the two politically opposed team members. The conflict starts as a disagreement over a workflow decision but quickly spirals into personal attacks tied to their ideological beliefs. Other team members grow visibly uncomfortable, avoiding eye contact and disengaging from the discussion. A junior employee, feeling overwhelmed by the hostility, later approaches Justin to express concerns about psychological safety and a lack of respect within the team. He comments that he has felt like the situation has been exacerbated by the company's sudden and unexplained deprioritization of DEI, and although he never viewed Justin as a DEI champion, he never thought he would let it get to this level of incivility.

This moment forces Justin to confront the impact of polarization and incivility on team dynamics. The conversation with the junior employee is a wake-up call, revealing the broader implications of these tensions on trust, collaboration, and morale.

Recognizing the urgency of the situation, Justin understands that showing empathy and understanding is crucial to bridging these divides. To tackle these issues head-on, he organizes an all-hands team meeting specifically designed to address the political tensions. Before the meeting, he prepares ground rules emphasizing respectful dialogue and sets clear expectations for engagement. During the meeting, Justin opens the floor for discussion, encouraging team members to share their thoughts and feelings while modeling vulnerability by expressing his own discomfort with the situation.

As tensions arise during discussions, Justin skillfully intervenes to guide conversations back to mutual respect. He employs techniques such as summarizing points of agreement and acknowledging differing opinions, reinforcing that all voices honoring the ground rules of respect will be heard. As a follow up to the all-hands, he establishes regular check-in sessions to maintain open lines of communication, allowing team members to continue sharing their experiences and concerns in a safe environment.

By encouraging his team members to express their perspectives in a structured and respectful manner, Justin demonstrates that he values their input—even when it differs from his own. Although this process is fraught with challenges, including moments of discomfort, he realizes that setting team norms that foster empathy is essential for maintaining cohesion and collaboration.

As conflicts deepen, Justin acknowledges that his ability to navigate these tensions is crucial—not just for the success of his team, but for the future of the company itself. In a climate where disagreements threaten to derail progress, the stakes are higher than ever. He must show his team that collaboration isn't just a company value on paper—it is essential for survival in a fast-changing market. Civility, in this context, becomes the foundation on which true inclusivity and progress depend.

Get Curious: What Just Happened?

Imagine you're on Justin's team as tensions boil over in a heated meeting. What starts as a disagreement over workflow quickly spirals into something deeper—personal attacks rooted in political and ideological differences. The room grows tense, some colleagues disengage, and a junior team member later expresses concerns about incivility on the team and psychological safety.

You watch as Justin takes it all in. His response in this moment will shape the team's ability to collaborate moving forward.

- How does Justin's response make you feel as a member of his team?
- What would you need from Justin at this moment to feel safe, respected, and engaged in your work?
- If you were in Justin's position, how would you have handled this situation?

Justin's journey underscores the impact of political and social polarization in the workplace. The conflict within his team revealed how unchecked ideological divides could erode trust, collaboration, and psychological safety. For Justin, addressing these tensions became a critical leadership challenge—not just to resolve conflict, but to safeguard the team's ability to innovate and thrive.

Using The Agency Loop to Overcome Polarization and Incivility

Leaders can leverage The Agency Loop to promote civil discourse by fostering environments where respectful dialogue becomes the norm. By aligning their values with intentional actions, leaders can transform moments of conflict into opportunities for deeper understanding and connection. Through this framework, leaders can create spaces that encourage open communication, empower diverse perspectives, and build trust, even in challenging situations.

To illustrate this approach, let's check in with Justin. We'll lean on his example, demonstrating how courageous leaders promote civil discourse in times of conflict by leaning into their values, controlling what they can, and finding meaning through experimentation.

Start with Authenticity

Justin demonstrates his commitment to creating space for civil discourse on his team by openly acknowledging the differing political perspectives within his team. He facilitates structured discussions where team members express their viewpoints respectfully, fostering an environment where every voice holds value. He models integrity by actively listening without judgment, reinforcing the importance of inclusivity and mutual respect.

To further this commitment, Justin commits to his team to establish a clear set of guidelines known as an "Inclusion Code." This code will outline the core values that underpin their interactions, such as "Disagree respectfully" and "Value differing opinions." By creating a space to build a shared understanding of these principles, Justin cultivates a culture that prioritizes respectful engagement, encouraging team members to uphold these values in all discussions.

Exercise Agency

Justin proactively shapes his team's communication environment. He collaborates with team members to refine the Inclusion Code, outlining expectations for respectful interactions, such as valuing differing opinions and listening to understand. He models these behaviors by actively listening without interruption and addressing breaches constructively, reinforcing the importance of maintaining respectful dialogue. He organizes structured sessions where all voices contribute, creating a safe space for open communication and mutual understanding.

Justin provides resources and training on effective communication and conflict resolution, equipping the team with essential skills. He conducts regular check-ins to reflect on communication dynamics, promoting continuous growth. Through these intentional actions, Justin creates a team culture that values and practices civil discourse, even amid differing viewpoints.

Embrace Growth

Justin views conflicts as opportunities for learning and development. He encourages his team to approach disagreements with curiosity, asking questions to understand underlying perspectives instead of making assumptions. He facilitates mini workshops on effective communication and conflict resolution during his staff meetings. He brings in experts to teach during larger organizational events, equipping all of his team members with tools to navigate differences constructively.

Justin implements regular reflection sessions where the team discusses recent conflicts, extracts lessons learned, and identifies strategies for future interactions. This continuous learning approach enhances individual skills and strengthens the team's collective ability to engage in civil discourse. By embracing diverse viewpoints and resolving conflicts constructively, Justin fosters a culture of growth and collaboration.

When the rise of political and social polarization triggers fear and uncertainty in your organization, courageous leaders find meaning in promoting civil discourse as a pathway to growth and innovation. By connecting this practice to a shared purpose—such as fostering inclusivity and mutual respect—leaders help their teams see conflict as an opportunity to learn and collaborate, rather than a source of division.

Leaders who embrace continuous learning create spaces for reflection and experimentation, strengthening their teams' ability to engage constructively. For instance, Justin's journey highlights the importance of proactively creating a culture of trust and mutual understanding. By offering resources, facilitating training, and regularly reflecting on lessons learned from conflicts, leaders demonstrate that civil discourse is more than a reaction to tension—it is a cornerstone of growth, resilience, and team cohesion.

Make It Matter

Now take a moment to think about your own workplace. Where do you see similar challenges? What opportunities do you have to lead with courage?

Use these questions to explore what this means for you:

- What stood out to you most about how Justin handled this situation? Why?
- Have you seen similar challenges in your own workplace? How did they play out?
- What's one way you could apply these insights in your leadership?
- What's one step—big or small—you can take this week to foster more civility and inclusion in your organization?

Case Study #3:
Addressing the Rapid Rise of Innovation

It's time to return to Taylor.

When we last left her, she had thought she was in the clear. Running The Agency Loop had helped her navigate the turbulence of launching the new AI platform, begin to rebuild trust with her team, and steady herself as a leader. She had wrestled with her own unease, fighting off the urge to let what she didn't know about the technology keep her from embracing it, and had chosen to step into the uncertainty rather than retreat from it. It hadn't been easy, but it had worked.

Yet here she was again, facing a new challenge that innovation had brought to her doorstep. The uncertainty she thought she had left behind was back—this time, in a different form. She was still wrestling with her own doubts about her leadership, rising to meet the moment even as the ground beneath her shifted.

As you read, put yourself on her team. What's working? What's not? Where does she step up, and where does she fall short? Most importantly, if you were on her team, what would you need from her as a leader? Because now, she had just received news that would change everything.

Her initial reaction was shock.

"What? You want me to take on another team?" Taylor's voice was steady, but the weight of the CDO's words pressed hard against her. She already had what was becoming a sprawling organization, and adding another team to it made her uneasy.

And it wasn't just any team.

Taylor was about to feel the full impact of the Nashville acquisition. The new team was based out of the company's newly acquired AI firm in Nashville and was part of a broader reorganization. For weeks, she had been working to rebuild trust with her current team after her initial hesitations about AI. Now because the company was moving so quickly, she barely had time to stabilize before being handed an entirely new group—one with its own culture, its own history, and its own expectations.

And just like that, the progress she had fought so hard for felt uncertain again.

Recognizing Dissonance: The Agency Loop Continues

She thought, *I just got back on my feet.* She immediately felt like she was going to have to start over with her team again. Bringing in new leaders and resetting expectations on how the team would operate was no small task, particularly because she knew this was a hostile acquisition. How could she expect her team to trust her when these changes kept coming without her knowing?

What made this situation even more precarious were the new AI tools that the team and the acquisition would bring, and how those tools had the potential to streamline processes and increase efficiency across her organization. There was no question that these tools and knowledge would make the whole team's job easier, but it would come at a cost. She knew that half of her organization, skilled in roles that AI could easily replace, was at risk of becoming obsolete.

She thought, confronting massive questions. *How can we leverage learning opportunities to build a future-ready, purpose-driven workforce while keeping the long-term needs of their people at the forefront? How can I keep my team moving forward when it seems like the directives keep coming, always with some new wrinkle?*

In a world where adaptability is the key to survival, the challenge was not just filling roles, but equipping her team with the skills and purpose to thrive in an ever-evolving landscape. And while she hadn't been given the directive to reduce her team size based on that potential, she recognized that she needs to act sooner rather than later to get out ahead of what that could mean for her team. Yet even though she knew she needed to act, a familiar feeling of dread started to creep in.

Get Curious: What Just Happened?

Before we dive into the next phase of Taylor's journey, let's get curious. Imagine you have a front-row seat to Taylor's reaction when she received the news that she was taking on a new team.

- How does Taylor's reaction to the AI-driven acquisition land with you? Does it make you feel more confident in her leadership, or does it raise concerns about how she is handling the change?
- If you were on her team, what would you need from Taylor to feel supported through this shift in the organization? How could she create psychological safety for employees facing uncertainty about AI and job security?
- If you were in Taylor's position, how would you have handled this transition? What's one step you would take to lead through the transition while maintaining trust with your team?

Taylor's experience highlights the complexity of leading in an era defined by rapid technological advancement and constant change. The acquisition of the Nashville AI firm brings both opportunity and challenge—new tools that promise to streamline processes and increase efficiency, while also raising concerns about workforce disruption. Taylor's initial reaction of shock and unease mirrors the tension many leaders feel when faced with integrating innovation while safeguarding trust and stability within their teams.

This moment underscores the broader theme of the chapter: how the rise of AI requires leaders to balance the promise of progress with the responsibility to prepare their teams for the future. Taylor recognizes that innovation must be paired with intentionality. While AI tools may simplify tasks, they also pose a risk to roles, creating anxiety among team members whose jobs are most vulnerable. She is acutely aware that her leadership during this period of transition will set the tone for whether her team feels empowered or alienated.

Courageous leaders understand that innovation is not just about adopting new technologies but about creating the conditions for people to thrive amid change. By proactively fostering learning opportunities, engaging in transparent communication, and building trust, Taylor has the opportunity to navigate this transition with both strategic foresight and humanity. The challenge lies not in the tools themselves but in ensuring her team feels valued and purpose-driven in an ever-evolving landscape.

Using The Agency Loop to Navigate Change in Innovation

Leaders can leverage The Agency Loop to navigate the challenges of innovation and change within their organization, specifically by reframing their approach from command and control to acting as the coach. By creating space for team skills to thrive to their team, finding durable skills that transcend the needs of the moment and focus on excellence through adaptation, leaders can build an environment where team members keep pace with the changing dynamics within organizations.

To illustrate this approach, we'll lean on Taylor's examples, demonstrating how courageous leaders build capabilities through coaching in moments of innovation by leaning into their values, controlling what they can, and finding meaning through experimentation.

When we first saw Taylor in this chapter, she was wrestling with the impending change coming from the addition of a new team bringing new skills and challenges. We asked you to put yourself in Taylor's shoes. Now it is time to see what she did.

Start with Authenticity

Taylor decided that to tackle this situation and the tension brought on by the moment, she needed to learn from her previous mistakes as a leader. First of all, she realized she needed to be herself, a human who recently came to terms with her own fear in the uncertainty of AI. She might not know how AI will impact her team, but she knew it was already creating change and could use that experience to help create space for her team members to also discuss their concerns and perspectives on the changes that may be coming. Her authenticity in moments of change helped build credibility and create space for her to manage the collective emotions of her team through building trust. That space also gave her the opportunity to get curious with her team members, using her own vulnerability to set them at ease.

She also recognizes that she needs to be a coach, and in doing so, she is going to have to be ready to deliver hard messages to help her team get ready for the change coming. She knows that she will be asked to share messages that support the company's acquisition decision. She also knows that while she'll get some information, there will likely be gaps where she doesn't have enough information, or that there may be sensitive information. She may know that sharing what she does know and admitting what she doesn't will likely put her in an uncomfortable position. This discomfort comes from the fact that she will likely cause her team members some pain and fear in the short term. But by maintaining her role as a coach, she can show courage here by facing her own discomfort and walking through it to set the stage for future growth.

Taylor knew she couldn't just sit back and wait for change to happen. She wanted to create space to confront her team's fears head-on. Taylor gathered her team members for an honest discussion about the potential impacts of AI on their roles. She didn't have all the answers, but she wanted them to know that their concerns mattered. "I understand that many of you are worried about what this means for your future," Taylor began. "And I am too. But I want us to navigate this together. We'll look for opportunities to learn new skills, adapt, and find ways for all of us to find value in our new tools as the company evolves." This transparency fostered a sense of collective purpose, and it helped alleviate some of the uncertainty they were feeling.

Taylor decided that her first step had to be listening—truly understanding what her team members felt about the upcoming changes and the impact on their roles. She initiated a series of one-on-one conversations, creating a safe space where her team members could express their fears and aspirations. "I want to know what matters most to you in this transition," she told them. These conversations revealed not only their concerns about obsolescence but their hopes for growth and new opportunities. By focusing on empathy, Taylor aimed to ensure her team felt supported and understood during this time of uncertainty.

She also knew that she needed to be ready to meet her own fear of confrontation if and when the time came to move forward with layoffs. She had fired people before for performance issues, but not in large numbers. She knew one of her former managers had navigated several layoffs who might be willing to work with her to get prepared. She reached out to begin talking through their experience and working on her approach.

Exercise Agency

Taylor knew she needed to better understand what skills were needed for the immediate integration of the two teams. She also knew she needed to be present for her team members, to listen to their fears and needs, while working with them to lay out next steps. By being a coach, she is forming two layers of connection— connecting her people to the work to be done and connecting herself to the team members in order to build trust.

Taylor knew she would need to accelerate the pace at which her team would adopt and find value in the new tools brought by the acquisition. For this to work, she knew that her team would need to explore how the new technology impacted their daily work. This meant exploring opportunities to automate or enhance their current work while also anticipating how the technology would reshape their roles over time.

Taylor asked the two teams to work together to create a shared understanding of their current capabilities. To do this, she paired team members with similar roles together, asking them to explore similarities and differences, discuss the current capabilities of the new tool, and for each member of the pair to share what their work meant to how the team creates value for the organization.

She set ground rules for the exercise that reflected her expectations of mutual respect and curiosity. This wasn't an exercise of comparing who was better, but an exploration of what is possible.

She brought the team back together a few days later to debrief. This was where she began the process of redefining the identity of the collective team. After giving the time for the pairs to report out, she asked the whole team to participate in a stop-start-continue exercise, looking at what they may need to stop work, where they may need to start new work, and what would continue forward through the change. This would form the basis of their collective action plan and the beginning of the new identity for the team.

Taylor has begun the process of identifying transferable skills, mapping out pathways for her team to transition into more stable roles within the company. Her focus isn't on simply keeping people employed but on aligning her team with a sense of purpose and giving them the tools to succeed in a world where adaptability and learning are the most valuable assets. This is her chance to shape her team's future, and she is determined to create opportunities for growth, not just survival. For Taylor, the opportunity isn't about replacing capabilities but expanding them, creating a purpose-driven team that is ready for the future.

Embrace Growth

She knows that the possibility for her team to experience layoffs is real. Because of that she needs to actively seek out opportunities within the organization to position her team members for potential roles. By being an advocate, she embodies her desire for her team to succeed in places that add value to the organization, laying the foundation for opportunity in face of potential layoffs.

She also knows that if she can determine the durable skills and capabilities her team needs to be successful in the long term, her team can navigate any new tool and change that comes her way in the future. By being a coach, she set the tone that the team should be able to navigate what the future holds, no matter what.

She knows that if she isn't able to avoid a layoff, she'll be tasked with terminating a portion of her team based on the new capabilities AI brings to her team and because of overlapping skills. She realizes that the integration of AI will likely automate some of the responsibilities on her team. Furthermore, with the merging of the team, she realizes that there are overlapping roles. She knows this will likely lead to a discussion with her leadership about how her organization can be tightened up when it comes time to reduce overhead in the acquisition.

For many managers, navigating this situation can be very difficult. Managers have to find the right way to navigate their responsibility to the company while still being true to what they believe. This is no different for Taylor. She may believe that every member of her team should be kept, that they all perform above company standards, or that the company is shortsighted to treat them as a number on a page rather than the humans that they are. We know that layoffs often have adverse effects on psychological safety within companies, and in this case, her team may experience those effects, particularly if she is asked to take from both her existing team and the new team she is inheriting.

She may not have the choice to keep the whole team, but Taylor does have the power to choose what she does in this situation that reflects her values as a coach. She has to have the courage to walk with the discomfort and, in turn, act in a way that brings her values to life.

As the team implemented their plan, Taylor held check-in meetings to discuss progress and challenges. In these check-ins she reinforced the collective identity and purpose that the team agreed upon, and took time to look for signs that the team needed space to process the losses of old ways of work. These signs came when team members' behavior changed and emotions stood out. Taylor approached these changes with curiosity and care, determining the best place to address those concerns. It was important to her to highlight where the team was letting go of past work and culture. By doing this she gave the team the opportunity to mourn the loss of identities and values that they had from before the change.

She also celebrated the process that they took, noting that what was most important was their practice in building the right behaviors.

In addition to the conversations and skill exploration, Taylor arranged for an interactive skills workshop, where her team could actively explore the training opportunities available to them. She worked with HR and other departments to ensure these workshops were not just about the skills needed for AI but also about building a growth mindset and fostering adaptability. This approach wasn't just about reskilling—it was about inspiring her team to see the potential within themselves and to understand that they had a place in the company's future.

But we want you to be the judge as part of Taylor's team. You're sitting in one of the reskilling sessions, and the conversation turns to the actions she has taken to prepare the team. Has she done enough to prepare the team?

- When Taylor made decisions with incomplete information, how would that affect your confidence in her leadership if you were on her team?
- How would her approach to balancing AI-driven innovation and job stability impact your sense of security on her team?
- As Taylor shifted from command-and-control leadership to a coaching approach, how would that change the way you interact with her as a team member?
- If you were in her shoes, what would you have done differently? What kind of leader would you have to be in this situation?

Make It Matter

Now take a moment to think about your own workplace. Where do you see similar challenges? What opportunities do you have to lead with courage?

Use these questions to explore what this means for you:

- What stood out to you most about how Taylor handled this situation? Why?
- Have you seen similar challenges in your own workplace? How did they play out?

- What's one way you could apply these insights in your leadership?
- What's one step—big or small—you can take this week to build coaching practices within your workplace?

Appendix 2: The Agency Loop Resources

Authenticity: Discovering Your Core Values for Courageous Leadership

Authenticity is the foundation of courageous leadership. To lead with courage, you need to know what drives you—your values, identity, and how they shape your leadership. This worksheet will help you define your core values and reflect on key aspects of your identity. Take your time with each part to get the most out of it!

Part 1: Discovering Your Core Values

Think about the values that guide your leadership. These values define what matters most to you and provide a compass for how you engage with the world.

1. **Select five values.** Choose the five values that resonate most from the list below. These are the values you strive to embody and align with in your leadership.

Leadership Values List

Integrity	Knowledge
Initiative	Optimism
Empathy	Humility
Dependability	Adaptability
Accountability	Vulnerability
Innovation	Excellence
Creativity	Fairness
Transparency	Inclusion
Collaboration	Accountability
Respect	Perseverance
Adaptability	Compassion
Self-Awareness	Agility
Gratitude	Strength
Commitment	Service
Loyalty	Loyalty
Authenticity	Determination
Patience	Equity
Diversity	Open-Mindedness
Decisiveness	

2. **Reflect on why these values matter.** Write down each value you selected and why it is important to you. Then answer these questions about each:

- List one way each value influences your actions, decisions, or relationships with your team.
- List one way each aligns with your leadership style. How does it shape how you lead—does it promote trust, resilience, or curiosity?

Part 2: Exploring Key Dimensions of Your Identity

Your identity is a critical component of your leadership. The unique combination of aspects of your identity shapes your perspective and influences how you lead.

1. **Select five to seven key dimensions of your identity.** Choose the dimensions that most influence your leadership. These may be cultural, personal, or professional and play a role in how you interact with others.

Cultural Background
Race
Ethnicity
Gender Identification
Age/Generation
Veteran Status
Socioeconomic Background
Family Role (e.g., Parent, Sibling, Caretaker)
Education

Professional Expertise/Role (e.g., Engineer, Manager, Consultant)
Religious or Spiritual Beliefs
Sexual Orientation
Political Beliefs
Health/Disability
Hobbies/Interests (e.g., Artist, Athlete, Musician)

Nationality
Immigrant Status
Regional/Local
   Identity (e.g., From
   a Certain Place or
   Community)
Personality Traits (e.g.,
   Introvert, Extrovert)
Life Experiences
   (e.g., Overcoming
   Adversity, Career
   Milestones)
Values (e.g., Integrity,
   Fairness, Service)
Leadership Style
   (e.g., Visionary,
   Empathetic,
   Directive)
Community or Social
   Engagement (e.g.,
   Volunteer, Activist)
Language/
   Communication
   Style

2. **Reflect on how these dimensions shape your leadership.**
    Write down each dimension you selected and why you
    selected it. Then answer these questions:

    - List one way each dimension of your identity affects
      your approach to leadership.
    - List one way each helps you build trust, foster collab-
      oration, or communicate more effectively.
    - List one way each of these aspects of your identity
      intersect and influence your leadership.

3. **Reflect on how your values and identity align.** Combine
    your lists. Then answer the following:

    - List one way your identity reinforces each of your
      values.

- List one way your values align with how you express your identity in your leadership.

Part 3: Seeing the Tension, Taking Action

Now that you've identified your core values and key aspects of your identity, it's time to explore how they interact with your current work environment. This next step is about curiosity—not judgment. The goal is to observe where your values and identity feel aligned with your environment and where they feel at odds.

1. **Identify the tension.** Take a few minutes to reflect on your day-to-day work environment and answer the following:

   - Where do you feel your values are supported and reinforced?
   - Where do you feel the tension where your values are challenged or ignored?
   - Which dimensions of your identity are salient (noticeable) when you experience this tension?

2. **Observe the tension in action.** Over the next week, pay close attention to moments when you feel either aligned or in tension with your values. Reflect on these questions:

   - What happened that made you feel aligned (or in tension) with your values?
   - How did you react? Did you adjust your behavior? Why?
   - How did this impact your leadership choices?

3. **Keeping a short daily note** on when you notice alignment or tension will help you spot patterns over time. Even quick bullet points can reveal insights about your leadership experience.

Part 4: Get Curious—Not Defensive

When you experience tension, your first instinct might be frustration. Remember a key component of authenticity is self-compassion. Show yourself some grace.

1. Consider these and write down your answers.

   - What is this tension trying to teach you?
   - Are you the only one feeling this, or do others experience it too?
   - What small step could you take to address this misalignment?

This exercise isn't about fixing everything immediately—it's about training yourself to see the moments where alignment and misalignment show up. The more you notice and analyze these moments, the more you will be able to navigate challenges, build trust, and create a meaningful impact within your team and organization.

Agency: Decision Calculus, Find Agency

Every decision you make as a leader is shaped by personal, professional, and situational factors. This worksheet helps you break down those elements so you can make choices that align with your values and leadership goals. Use it for big and small decisions—the more you practice, the clearer your path becomes.

Part 1: Identify the Situation

Think about a current situation where you have to make an important decision. Write down the answers to the following questions to better understand the situation.

- What is the situation?
- Is there any additional relevant context?

Part 2: Mine for Agency

Think about the possible actions you could take in this situation. Be real with yourself. Challenge your assumptions about the situations. Then answer the following:.

- What actions are in your control? List your options.
- What do you have the ability to influence, even in small ways? List your options.
- How can you align your actions with your core values here?
- What choices are you free to make right now? List your options.
- Are there beliefs about the situation and your choices that you are willing to challenge that may not be true?

Part 3: Factor in Your Privilege

Think about how your privilege might shape your decision about the options you listed above. Consider things like financial security, title, or social advantages and how they might influence your options. Write down the answers to the following questions to better understand the role privilege is playing in your situation.

- What privileges or advantages do you have that may influence your decision?
- What disadvantages do you have that you should take into account?

Part 4: Evaluate the Risks

What's at stake for you, your team, or the organization? Revisit the options you listed above and list both the immediate impact and the long-term consequences of each. Then answer the following:

- What will you lose if you act (reputation, relationships, security)?
- What could you gain by acting (integrity, trust, alignment)?
- What will you lose by not acting?
- What might you gain by staying silent or avoiding action?

Part 5: Acknowledge Your Fear

Fear is part of the process. Consider what's holding you back from taking the action that aligns with your values. Then answer the following:

- What fears come up when I think about taking action?
- Are these fears based on real consequences, or are they assumptions?
- How can I address these fears without letting them control my decision?

Part 6: Work the Equation

Look at the whole picture. That is your decision calculus. Consider the balance between your agency, your privilege, the stakes, and your fear. Then answer the following:

- Where do you stand now?
- What is the most important variable in your decision calculus?
- What feels like the most aligned action, given all these factors?
- Is there a small step you can take to move forward in the right direction, even if it's not a perfect solution?
- How can you move through this decision with intention, even if you don't have all the answers?

Part 7: Decide on Your Decision

You worked your calculus; now make the decision. Then answer the following:

- What is your decision?
- Are you acting from a place of courage and authenticity?
- What does this decision say about you as a leader?

Part 8: Take Action

Take the action that aligns with your values and commitment to leading with courage. This exercise isn't about making perfect decisions every time—it's about building the habit of recognizing the factors at play in your choices. The more you practice breaking down decisions, the better you'll align your actions with your values, navigate complexity with confidence, and lead with clarity and impact.

Growth: Making Meaning Using the Appreciation Questions

The Appreciation Questions are designed to help you reflect on your decisions and actions as a leader. They offer a space to look back at moments where there may have been a gap between your intended and experienced outcomes. This process allows you to extract valuable lessons from those moments, as well as the meaning behind the emotions you experienced. Use these questions to make sense of impactful moments in your leadership journey, helping you turn those experiences into actionable insights for continued growth.

Reflect on a leadership moment where the outcome differed from your expectations. Use the Appreciation Questions to explore what you learned, the emotions you felt, and how this experience can inform your growth. Focus on turning this reflection into actionable insights that will strengthen your leadership moving forward.

- What was the moment that mattered?
- What was the tension or dissonance in the experience?
- What were the expected / intended outcomes?
- What was the actual outcome?
- What were the consequences of the outcome?
- What emotions came from the experience?
- What do the outcomes and consequences mean *to* you?
- What do the outcomes and consequences mean *for* you?

Stuck? To help illustrate how these questions can be applied, we've used "Mike's Moment That Mattered: Fired" from the beginning of chapter 4 to demonstrate how he used the Appreciation Questions to find the meaning in this specific experience. Review it as a guide to help you work through your own questions.

Question	What Was Happening?	Mike's Answers
What was the Moment That Matters?	Recognition of moment when tension happened	• Being fired from that same role after significant organizational change
What was the tension or dissonance in the experience?	Recognition of what emotions and conflict emerged as part of the experience	• Sudden departure of HR leader with little warning in the first week • Fired for lack of performance
What were the expected / intended outcomes?	Exploration of aim and variables included in the calculus	• Demonstrate leadership at the highest level • Personal and career growth • Making meaningful change in the company • Stabilize the team
What was the actual outcome?	Establishing outcome to create space to identify the gap between intended and actual outcomes	• Program was implemented within the time frame at the expense of other projects • Departure of the HR leader destabilized the role • Fired for performance because of the deprioritized project
What were the consequences of the outcome?	Exploring the impact of the outcomes	• Short-term consequences: Burnout, emotional and physical strain, and breakdown of identity as leader • Long-term consequences: Forced reevaluation of leadership identity and personal values, including the value placed on personal value alignment with organizational values • Career consequences: Anticipation of the forced exit allowed for the development of an exit strategy, but did not give time and space to address deeper personal impact
What emotions came from the experience?	Recognition of the full spectrum of emotions in the outcome and consequences	• In the beginning: Excitement, optimism, and pride in taking on a high-stakes leadership role • When the tension increased: Anxiety, frustration, and uncertainty from leadership change and the growing tension in the role • After being fired: Shock, shame, self-doubt, and grief over the perceived loss of identity, with lingering resentment and confusion about the circumstances

Question	What Was Happening?	Mike's Answers
What do the outcomes and consequences mean to me?	Identification of the impact the whole experience has on a leader	• The experience reinforced the concept that as leaders, we can only truly control how we respond in Moments That Matter • It underscored the fragility of identity when tied too closely to external validation, like a job title or an organization • Brought to light the cost of unresolved tension, both physical and emotional
What do the outcomes and consequences mean for me?	Beginning to take the impact and develop a picture of how the outcomes change the leader	• Reinforces commitment as a leader to be transparent, candid, and intentional when working with team members • Expands the calculus of risk and how that risk aligns with personal identities • Helps refine what values mean (e.g., what it means to be the kid who always hustles versus putting energy into the right areas that align with personal values)

After seeing how Mike navigated his moment, revisit the Appreciation Questions to reflect on your own experiences. Think about how Mike's process of reflection and learning can inform the way you make meaning out of your most important moments. Consider how identifying gaps between your intended and actual outcomes can lead to valuable insights, and how you can use those insights to turn challenges into growth opportunities. The Appreciation Questions help create the space for that reflection and learning, empowering you to grow from your own leadership moments.

Glossary

Adaptation: An element of the growth phase; the ability to integrate the parts and pieces of lessons learned.

Agency: The ability to make intentional decisions based on your values.

The Agency Loop: A practical approach to managing how you respond to conflict between your values and your environment.

Appreciation: An element of the growth phase; the ability to take full stock of the experience and the consequences of your actions.

Authenticity: The ability to align who you are with how you show up in the world.

Courage: The resolve to face fear or uncertainty, guided by care for what truly matters.

Courageous leadership: The ability to act based on your values in the face of fear.

Curiosity: Openness to self-discovery and exploring others' perspectives.

Decisiveness: An element of the agency phase; the ability to make clear, confident decisions that align with your values and priorities.

Dissonance: A conflict between your values and your environment.

Growth: The ability to learn, adapt, and evolve through your experiences.

Inner game: Your mindset, values, emotional resilience, and authenticity—how you handle challenges internally.

Intentionality: An element of the agency phase; the ability to act in a deliberate way with a certain outcome in mind.

Loop: A continuous cycle of action, reflection, and growth through repeated practice and adaptation.

Moment That Matters: When you make meaning of an experience that caused tension.

Outer game: The actions you take—leading decisively, taking risks, and making choices that align with your inner values.

Resilience: The ability to adapt and bounce back from challenges.

Self-compassion: An element of the authenticity phase; the ability to extend kindness to yourself when you fall short of expectations.

Tension: An emotional, mental, or physical experience that causes dissonance.

Trigger: The recognition of the dissonance that activates The Agency Loop.

Trust: Belief in yourself and inspiring confidence through integrity and consistency.

Vulnerability: An element of the authenticity phase; the ability to question yourself and dig deep for answers.

Endnotes

Chapter 1

1 Brené Brown, *I Thought It Was Just Me (But It Isn't): Making the Journey from "What Will People Think?" to "Am I Enough?"* (New York: Random House, 2007), xxiii.

2 Robert Ellis, *Coaching From Essence: Create a Thriving Practice Doing Powerful Work with Clients You Love* (Futurosity, 2023), 31–35.

3 Manfred F. R. Kets de Vries, "How to Find and Practice Courage," *Harvard Business Review*, May 2020, https://hbr.org/2020/05/how-to-find-and-practice-courage.

4 Valerie Workman, "Bringing My Whole Self to Work at Tesla," *LinkedIn*, May 2020, https://www.linkedin.com/pulse/bringing-my-whole-self-work-tesla-valerie-workman-esq-/.

5 Frank Herbert, *Dune* (New York: Ace Books, 2005), 10.

6 Herbert, *Dune,* 10.

7 Brené Brown, *Dare to Lead: Brave Work. Tough Conversations. Whole Hearts* (New York: Random House, 2018), 192.

Chapter 2

1   Karissa Thacker, *The Art of Authenticity: Tools to Become an Authentic Leader and Your Best Self* (San Francisco: Berrett-Koehler Publishers, 2018), 44.

2   Thacker, *The Art of Authenticity,* 66–67.

3   Kimberlé Crenshaw, "Demarginalizing the Intersection of Race and Sex: A Black Feminist Critique of Antidiscrimination Doctrine, Feminist Theory, and Antiracist Politics," *University of Chicago Legal Forum* 1989, no. 1 (1989): 139–167.

4   Michael Hecht and Kaitlin Phillips, "The Communication Theory of Identity," in *The Routledge Handbook of Applied Communication Research,* ed. H. Dan O'Hair and Mary John O'Hair (New York: Routledge, 2020), 221–232.

5   Ellis, *Coaching from Essence,* 31–35.

6   Kenji Yoshino, *Covering: The Hidden Assault on Our Civil Rights* (New York: Random House, 2006), 18.

7   Bill George, et al. "Discovering Your Authentic Leadership," *Harvard Business Review*, February 2007, https://hbr.org/2007/02/discovering-your-authentic-leadership.

8   Rich Fernandez and Steph Stern, "How Self-Compassion Will Make You a Better Leader," *Harvard Business Review* webinar, February 2021, https://hbr.org/webinar/2021/02/how-self-compassion-will-make-you-a-better-leader.

9   Kristin D. Neff, "Self-Compassion: Theory, Method, Research, and Intervention," *Annual Review of Psychology* 74 (2023): 193–218, https://www.annualreviews.org/content/journals/10.1146/annurev-psych-032420-031047.

Chapter 3

1   Viktor E. Frankl, *Man's Search for Meaning* (Boston: Beacon Press, 2006), 65–69.

2   PwC, *Hopes and Fears Survey* (June 24, 2024), https://www.pwc.com/gx/en/issues/workforce/hopes-and-fears.html.

3   Merriam-Webster, s.v. "manipulation," accessed February 21, 2025, https://www.merriam-webster.com/dictionary/manipulation.

4   Kimberlé Crenshaw, "Mapping the Margins: Intersectionality, Identity Politics, and Violence against Women of Color," *Stanford Law Review* 43, no. 6 (1991): 1241–1299.

Chapter 4

1   Daniel Kahneman, *Thinking, Fast and Slow*. New York: Farrar, Straus and Giroux, 2011.

2   John P. Kotter, *Change: How Organizations Achieve Hard-to-Imagine Results in Uncertain and Volatile Times* (New York: Ideapress Publishing, 2021), 19–21.

3   Carol S. Dweck, *Mindset: The New Psychology of Success* (New York: Ballantine Books, 2016), 132.

4   Merriam-Webster, s.v. "appreciation," accessed February 21, 2025, https://www.merriam-webster.com/dictionary/appreciation#:~:text=%3A%20 a%20feeling%20or%20expression%20of,small%20token%20of%20our%20 appreciation.

5   Abraham H. Maslow, *Motivation and Personality* (New York: Harper & Row, 1954), 34–58.

6   Elisabeth Kübler-Ross, *On Death and Dying: 50th Anniversary Edition* (New York: Scribner, 2019), 109–116.

7   James Clear, *Atomic Habits: An Easy & Proven Way to Build Good Habits & Break Bad Ones* (New York: Avery, 2018), 212–213.

8   Charles Duhigg, *The Power of Habit: Why We Do What We Do in Life and Business* (New York: Random House, 2012), 287–298.

9   Vanessa Shaw, conversation with the author, March, 2023, https://momentouswork.com/.

10   William Bridges and Susan Bridges, *Managing Transitions: Making the Most of Change*, 4th ed. (Boston: Da Capo Lifelong Books, 2017), 32–34.

Chapter 5

1   World Uncertainty Index, accessed February 21, 2025, https://worlduncertaintyindex.com/.

2   Edelman, *2024 Edelman Trust Barometer* (Edelman, 2024), accessed February 21, 2025, https://www.edelman.com/trust/2024/trust-barometer.

3   Nathaniel Fast, Nir Halevy, and Selin Kesebir, "Why We Prefer Dominant Leaders in Uncertain Times," *Harvard Business Review*, August 2017, https://hbr.org/2017/08/why-we-prefer-dominant-leaders-in-uncertain-times.

4   Deloitte, *Human Capital Trends Report* (2024), accessed February 21, 2025, https://www2.deloitte.com/us/en/insights/focus/human-capital-trends.html.

5   Gallup, *State of the Global Workplace Report* (2024), accessed February 21, 2025, https://www.gallup.com/workplace/349484/state-of-the-global-workplace.aspx.

6   Mercer, *Global Talent Trends Report* (2024), accessed February 21, 2025, https://www.mercer.com/en-ae/insights/people-strategy/future-of-work/global-talent-trends/.

7   Gartner, *Top Priorities for HR Leaders* (2024), accessed February 21, 2025, https://www.gartner.com/en/human-resources/trends/top-priorities-for-hr-leaders.

8   Gartner, *Top Priorities for HR Leaders*.

Chapter 6

1   US Census Bureau, *2017 National Population Projections Summary Tables*, accessed February 21, 2025, https://www.census.gov/data/tables/2017/demo/popproj/2017-summary-tables.html.

2   Target Corporation, *Belonging at the Bullseye Strategy*, January 2025, https://corporate.target.com/press/fact-sheet/2025/01/belonging-bullseye-strategy.

3   John Deere (@JohnDeere), "Our customers' trust and confidence . . .," *X (formerly Twitter)*, July 16, 2024, https://x.com/JohnDeere/status/1813318977650847944.

4   Harley-Davidson (@harleydavidson), "We remain committed to . . . ,"
     X (formerly Twitter), August 19, 2024, https://x.com/harleydavidson/
     status/1825564138032234994.

5   McDonald's Corporation, *Our Commitment to Inclusion*, accessed February
     21, 2025, https://corporate.mcdonalds.com/corpmcd/our-stories/article/
     our-commitment-to-inclusion.html.

6   Anne D'Innocenzio, "Walmart DEI Inclusion Diversity," *Associated
     Press News*, November 25, 2024, https://apnews.com/article/
     walmart-dei-inclusion-diversity-34b06922e60e5116fe198696201ce4d9.

7   Tractor Supply Company, *Tractor Supply Company Statement*, news release,
     2024, https://corporate.tractorsupply.com/newsroom/news-releases/news-
     releases-details/2024/Tractor-Supply-Company-Statement/default.aspx.

8   Apple Inc., *DEF 14A Proxy Statement*, US Securities and Exchange
     Commission, filed January 10, 2025, https://www.sec.gov/ix?doc=/
     Archives/edgar/data/320193/000130817925000008/aapl4359751-def14a.
     htm.

9   Costco Wholesale Corporation, *SEC Filing*, US Securities and Exchange
     Commission, filed December 11, 2024, https://www.sec.gov/Archives/
     edgar/data/909832/000090983224000072/cost-20241209.htm.

10   Marc J. Dunkelman, *The Vanishing Neighbor: The Transformation of American
     Community* (New York: W.W. Norton & Company, 2014), 97–98.

11   Thomas F. Pettigrew, et al. "Recent Advances in Intergroup Contact Theory,"
     International Journal of Intercultural Relations 35, no. 3 (2011): 271–280,
     https://doi.org/10.1016/j.ijintrel.2011.03.001.

12   Dunkelman, *The Vanishing Neighbor*, 134–138.

13   Nathaniel Fast, Nir Halevy, and Selin Kesebir, "Why We
     Prefer Dominant Leaders in Uncertain Times," *Harvard
     Business Review*, August 2017, https://hbr.org/2017/08/
     why-we-prefer-dominant-leaders-in-uncertain-times.

14   Amy C. Edmondson, "Psychological Safety and Learning Behavior in
     Work Teams," *Administrative Science Quarterly* 44, no. 2 (1999): 350–383,
     https://web.mit.edu/curhan/www/docs/Articles/15341_Readings/Group_
     Performance/Edmondson%20Psychological%20safety.pdf.

Chapter 7

1 Fast, Halevy, and Kesebir, "Why We Prefer Dominant Leaders."

2 Society for Human Resource Management (SHRM), *Civility Index Q3 2024* (2024), https://www.shrm.org/topics-tools/topics/civility.

3 Angelo Mendoza, "Political Differences in the Workplace," *Indeed Career Advice*, accessed February 21, 2025, https://www.indeed.com/career-advice/news/political-differences-workplace.

4 Rachel Kleinfeld, *Polarization, Democracy, and Political Violence in the United States: What the Research Says* (Washington, DC: Carnegie Endowment for International Peace, 2023), https://carnegieendowment.org/research/2023/09/polarization-democracy-and-political-violence-in-the-united-states-what-the-research-says?lang=en.

5 Shanto Iyengar, et al. "The Origins and Consequences of Affective Polarization in the United States," *Annual Review of Political Science* 22 (2019): 129–146, https://www.annualreviews.org/content/journals/10.1146/annurev-polisci-051117-073034.

6 SHRM, *Civility Index Q3 2024*.

7 Porath and Pearson, "The Price of Incivility."

8 Julia Minson and Francesca Gino, "Managing a Polarized Workforce," *Harvard Business Review*, March 2022, https://hbr.org/2022/03/managing-a-polarized-workforce.

Chapter 8

1 World Intellectual Property Organization (WIPO), *Global Innovation Index 2024* (2024), accessed February 21, 2025, https://www.wipo.int/web-publications/global-innovation-index-2024/en/.

2 Barry Jaruzelski, Robert Chwalik, and Brad Goehle, "What the Top Innovators Get Right." *Strategy+Business*. Accessed February 21, 2025. https://www.strategy-business.com/feature/What-the-Top-Innovators-Get-Right.

3 WIPO, *Global Innovation Index 2024*.

4   KPMG, *Global Tech Report 2024* (2024), accessed February 21, 2025, https://kpmg.com/xx/en/our-insights/transformation/kpmg-global-tech-report-2024.html.

5   Sam Gustin, "The Fatal Mistake That Doomed BlackBerry," *TIME*, September 24, 2013, https://business.time.com/2013/09/24/the-fatal-mistake-that-doomed-blackberry/.

6   Kari Paul, "How BlackBerry Went from a Status Symbol to a Punchline," *The Guardian*, October 15, 2023, https://www.theguardian.com/technology/2023/oct/15/blackberry-smartphone-status-symbol-then-crashed-and-burned.

7   McKinsey & Company, *The State of AI* (2024), accessed February 21, 2025, https://www.mckinsey.com/capabilities/quantumblack/our-insights/the-state-of-ai.

8   KPMG, *Generative AI Survey* (August 2024), accessed February 21, 2025, https://kpmg.com/us/en/media/news/gen-ai-survey-august-2024.html.

9   Mercer, *Global Talent Trends Report*.

10 ADP Research Institute, *People at Work 2024: A Global Workforce View* (2024), accessed February 21, 2025, https://www.adpresearch.com/assets/summary-of-people-at-work-2024-a-global-workforce-view/.

11 Christoph Riedl, "How to Use AI to Build Your Company's Collective Intelligence," *Harvard Business Review*, October 2024, https://hbr.org/2024/10/how-to-use-ai-to-build-your-companys-collective-intelligence.

12 Kotter, *Change*, 31.

13 Josh Bersin, *Irresistible: The Seven Secrets of the World's Most Enduring, Employee-Focused Organizations* (Oakland, CA: Berrett-Koehler Publishers, 2022), 44.

14 Microsoft, *Work Trend Index 2024* (2024), accessed February 21, 2025, https://news.microsoft.com/annual-wti-2024/.

15 Dweck, *Mindset*, 140.

16 Bersin, *Irresistible*, 77–105.

17 Tony Dungy, *The Mentor Leader: Secrets to Building People and Teams That Win Consistently* (Carol Stream, IL: Tyndale House Publishers, 2010).

18   Phil Jackson and Hugh Delehanty, *Eleven Rings: The Soul of Success* (New York: Penguin Press, 2013).

19   Pat Summitt, *Reach for the Summit: The Definite Dozen System for Succeeding at Whatever You Do* (New York: Broadway Books, 1998).

20   Luc de Brabandere, *The Forgotten Half of Change: Achieving Greater Creativity Through Changes in Perception* (Chicago: Kaplan Publishing, 2005), 43.

Bibliography

1. ADP Research Institute. *People at Work 2024: A Global Workforce View*. 2024. Accessed February 21, 2025. https://www.adpresearch.com/assets/ summary-of-people-at-work-2024-a-global-workforce-view/.

2. Apple Inc. *DEF 14A Proxy Statement*. US Securities and Exchange Commission. Filed January 10, 2025. https://www.sec.gov/ix?doc=/ Archives/edgar/data/320193/000130817925000008/aapl4359751-def14a. htm.

3. Ben-Ghiat, Ruth. *Strongmen: How They Rise, Why They Succeed, How They Fall*. New York: W.W. Norton & Company, 2020.

4. Bersin, Josh. *Irresistible: The Seven Secrets of the World's Most Enduring, Employee-Focused Organizations*. Oakland, CA: Berrett-Koehler Publishers, 2022.

5. Brabandere, Luc de. *The Forgotten Half of Change: Achieving Greater Creativity Through Changes in Perception*. Chicago: Kaplan Publishing, 2005.

6. Bridges, William, and Susan Bridges. *Managing Transitions: Making the Most of Change*. 4th ed. Boston: Da Capo Lifelong Books, 2017.

7. Brown, Brené. *Braving the Wilderness: The Quest for True Belonging and the Courage to Stand Alone*. New York: Random House, 2017.

8. ———. *Dare to Lead: Brave Work. Tough Conversations. Whole Hearts*. New York: Random House, 2018.

9. ———. *I Thought It Was Just Me (But It Isn't): Making the Journey from "What Will People Think?" to "Am I Enough?"* New York: Random House, 2007.

10. Clear, James. *Atomic Habits: An Easy & Proven Way to Build Good Habits & Break Bad Ones.* New York: Avery, 2018.

11. Costco Wholesale Corporation. *SEC Filing.* US Securities and Exchange Commission. Filed December 11, 2024. https://www.sec.gov/Archives/edgar/data/909832/000090983224000072/cost-20241209.htm.

12. Crenshaw, Kimberlé. "Demarginalizing the Intersection of Race and Sex: A Black Feminist Critique of Antidiscrimination Doctrine, Feminist Theory, and Antiracist Politics." *University of Chicago Legal Forum* 1989, no. 1 (1989): 139–167.

13. ———. "Mapping the Margins: Intersectionality, Identity Politics, and Violence against Women of Color." *Stanford Law Review* 43, no. 6 (1991): 1241–1299.

14. Deloitte. *Human Capital Trends Report.* 2024. Accessed February 21, 2025. https://www2.deloitte.com/us/en/insights/focus/human-capital-trends.html.

15. D'Innocenzio, Anne. "Walmart DEI Inclusion Diversity." *Associated Press News*, November 25, 2024. https://apnews.com/article/walmart-dei-inclusion-diversity-34b06922e60e5116fe198696201ce4d9.

16. Duhigg, Charles. *The Power of Habit: Why We Do What We Do in Life and Business.* New York: Random House, 2012.

17. Dungy, Tony. *The Mentor Leader: Secrets to Building People and Teams That Win Consistently.* Carol Stream, IL: Tyndale House Publishers, 2010.

18. Dunkelman, Marc J. *The Vanishing Neighbor: The Transformation of American Community.* New York: W.W. Norton & Company, 2014.

19. Dweck, Carol S. *Mindset: The New Psychology of Success.* New York: Ballantine Books, 2016.

20. Edelman. *2024 Edelman Trust Barometer.* Edelman, 2024. Accessed February 21, 2025. https://www.edelman.com/trust/2024/trust-barometer.

21. Edmondson, Amy C. *The Fearless Organization: Creating Psychological Safety in the Workplace for Learning, Innovation, and Growth*. Hoboken, NJ: Wiley, 2019.

22. Edmondson, Amy C. "Psychological Safety and Learning Behavior in Work Teams." *Administrative Science Quarterly* 44, no. 2 (1999): 350–383. https://web.mit.edu/curhan/www/docs/Articles/15341_Readings/Group_Performance/Edmondson%20Psychological%20safety.pdf.

23. Ellis, Robert. *Coaching From Essence: Create a Thriving Practice Doing Powerful Work with Clients You Love*. Futurosity, 2023.

24. Fast, Nathaniel, Nir Halevy, and Selin Kesebir. "Why We Prefer Dominant Leaders in Uncertain Times." *Harvard Business Review*, August 2017. https://hbr.org/2017/08/why-we-prefer-dominant-leaders-in-uncertain-times.

25. Fernandez, Rich, and Steph Stern. "How Self-Compassion Will Make You a Better Leader." *Harvard Business Review* webinar, February 2021. https://hbr.org/webinar/2021/02/how-self-compassion-will-make-you-a-better-leader.

26. Frankl, Viktor E. *Man's Search for Meaning*. Boston: Beacon Press, 2006.

27. Gallup. *State of the Global Workplace Report*. 2024. Accessed February 21, 2025. https://www.gallup.com/workplace/349484/state-of-the-global-workplace.aspx.

28. Gartner. *Top Priorities for HR Leaders*. 2024. Accessed February 21, 2025. https://www.gartner.com/en/human-resources/trends/top-priorities-for-hr-leaders.

29. George, Bill. *Authentic Leadership: Rediscovering the Secrets to Creating Lasting Value*. San Francisco: Jossey-Bass, 2003.

30. ———. *True North: Leading Authentically in Today's Workplace, Emerging Leader Edition*. Hoboken, NJ: Wiley, 2022.

31. George, Bill, Peter Sims, Andrew N. McLean, and Diana Mayer. "Discovering Your Authentic Leadership." *Harvard Business Review*, February 2007. https://hbr.org/2007/02/discovering-your-authentic-leadership.

32. Gustin, Sam. "The Fatal Mistake That Doomed BlackBerry." *TIME*, September 24, 2013. https://business.time.com/2013/09/24/the-fatal-mistake-that-doomed-blackberry/.

33. Harley-Davidson (@harleydavidson), "We remain committed to . . . ," *X (formerly Twitter)*, August 19, 2024, https://x.com/harleydavidson/status/1825564138032234994.

34. Hecht, Michael, and Kaitlin Phillips. "The Communication Theory of Identity." In *The Routledge Handbook of Applied Communication Research*, edited by H. Dan O'Hair and Mary John O'Hair, 221–232. New York: Routledge, 2020.

35. Heifetz, Ronald A., Marty Linsky, and Alexander Grashow. *The Practice of Adaptive Leadership: Tools and Tactics for Changing Your Organization and the World*. Boston: Harvard Business Press, 2009.

36. Herbert, Frank. *Dune*. New York: Ace Books, 2005.

37. Iyengar, Shanto, Yphtach Lelkes, Matthew Levendusky, Neil Malhotra, and Sean J. Westwood. "The Origins and Consequences of Affective Polarization in the United States." *Annual Review of Political Science* 22 (2019): 129–146. https://www.annualreviews.org/content/journals/10.1146/annurev-polisci-051117-073034.

38. Jackson, Phil, and Hugh Delehanty. *Eleven Rings: The Soul of Success*. New York: Penguin Press, 2013.

39. Jaruzelski, Barry, Robert Chwalik, and Brad Goehle, "What the Top Innovators Get Right." *Strategy+Business*. Accessed February 21, 2025. https://www.strategy-business.com/feature/What-the-Top-Innovators-Get-Right.

40. John Deere (@JohnDeere), "Our customers' trust and confidence . . . ," *X (formerly Twitter)*, July 16, 2024, https://x.com/JohnDeere/status/1813318977650847944.

41. Kahneman, Daniel. *Thinking, Fast and Slow*. New York: Farrar, Straus and Giroux, 2011.

42. Kets de Vries, Manfred F. R. "How to Find and Practice Courage." *Harvard Business Review*, May 2020. https://hbr.org/2020/05/how-to-find-and-practice-courage.

43. Kleinfeld, Rachel. *Polarization, Democracy, and Political Violence in the United States: What the Research Says*. Washington, DC: Carnegie Endowment for International Peace, 2023. https://carnegieendowment.org/research/2023/09/polarization-democracy-and-political-violence-in-the-united-states-what-the-research-says?lang=en.

44. Kotter, John P. *Change: How Organizations Achieve Hard-to-Imagine Results in Uncertain and Volatile Times*. New York: Ideapress Publishing, 2021.

45. KPMG. *Generative AI Survey* (August 2024). Accessed February 21, 2025, https://kpmg.com/us/en/media/news/gen-ai-survey-august-2024.html.

46. ———. *Global Tech Report 2024*. 2024. Accessed February 21, 2025. https://kpmg.com/xx/en/our-insights/transformation/kpmg-global-tech-report-2024.html.

47. Kübler-Ross, Elisabeth. *On Death and Dying: 50th Anniversary Edition*. New York: Scribner, 2019.

48. Lencioni, Patrick. *The Five Dysfunctions of a Team: A Leadership Fable*. San Francisco: Jossey-Bass, 2002.

49. Maslow, Abraham H. *Motivation and Personality*. New York: Harper & Row, 1954.

50. McDonald's Corporation. *Our Commitment to Inclusion*. Accessed February 21, 2025. https://corporate.mcdonalds.com/corpmcd/our-stories/article/our-commitment-to-inclusion.html.

51. McKinsey & Company. *The State of AI* (2024). Accessed February 21, 2025, https://www.mckinsey.com/capabilities/quantumblack/our-insights/the-state-of-ai.

52. Mendoza, Angelo. "Political Differences in the Workplace." *Indeed Career Advice*. Accessed February 21, 2025. https://www.indeed.com/career-advice/news/political-differences-workplace.

53. Mercer. *Global Talent Trends Report*. 2024. Accessed February 21, 2025. https://www.mercer.com/en-ae/insights/people-strategy/future-of-work/global-talent-trends/.

54. Merriam-Webster. s.v. "appreciation." Accessed February 21, 2025. https://www.merriam-webster.com/dictionary/appreciation.

55. ———. s.v. "manipulation." Accessed February 21, 2025. https://www. merriam-webster.com/dictionary/manipulation.

56. Microsoft. *Work Trend Index 2024* (2024). Accessed February 21, 2025, https://news.microsoft.com/annual-wti-2024/.

57. Minson, Julia, and Francesca Gino. "Managing a Polarized Workforce." *Harvard Business Review*, March 2022. https://hbr.org/2022/03/ managing-a-polarized-workforce.

58. Neff, Kristin D. "Self-Compassion: Theory, Method, Research, and Intervention." *Annual Review of Psychology* 74 (2023): 193–218. https://www.annualreviews.org/content/journals/10.1146/ annurev-psych-032420-031047.

59. Paul, Kari. "How BlackBerry Went from a Status Symbol to a Punchline." *The Guardian*, October 15, 2023. https:// www.theguardian.com/technology/2023/oct/15/ blackberry-smartphone-status-symbol-then-crashed-and-burned.

60. Pettigrew, Thomas F., Linda R. Tropp, Ulrich Wagner, and Oliver Christ. "Recent Advances in Intergroup Contact Theory." *International Journal of Intercultural Relations* 35, no. 3 (2011): 271–280. https://doi.org/10.1016/j. ijintrel.2011.03.001.

61. Porath, Christine, and Christine Pearson. "The Price of Incivility." *Harvard Business Review*, January 2013. https://hbr.org/2013/01/ the-price-of-incivility.

62. PwC. *Hopes and Fears Survey*. June 24, 2024. https://www.pwc.com/gx/en/ issues/workforce/hopes-and-fears.html.

63. Riedl, Christoph. "How to Use AI to Build Your Company's Collective Intelligence." *Harvard Business Review*, October 2024. https://hbr. org/2024/10/how-to-use-ai-to-build-your-companys-collective-intelligence.

64. Senge, Peter M. *The Fifth Discipline: The Art & Practice of the Learning Organization*. New York: Doubleday, 1990.

65. Shanto, Iyengar, Yphtach Lelkes, Matthew Levendusky, Neil Malhotra, and Sean J. Westwood. "The Origins and Consequences of Affective Polarization in the United States." *Annual Review of Political Science* 22 (2019): 129–146. https://www.annualreviews.org/content/journals/10.1146/ annurev-polisci-051117-073034.

66. Shaw, Vanessa. Conversation with the author, March 2023. https://momentouswork.com/.

67. Smith, David Livingstone. *On Inhumanity: Dehumanization and How to Resist It*. New York: Oxford University Press, 2020.

68. Society for Human Resource Management (SHRM). *Civility Index Q3 2024*. 2024. https://www.shrm.org/topics-tools/topics/civility.

69. Summitt, Pat. *Reach for the Summit: The Definite Dozen System for Succeeding at Whatever You Do*. New York: Broadway Books, 1998.

70. Target Corporation. *Belonging at the Bullseye Strategy*. January 2025. https://corporate.target.com/press/fact-sheet/2025/01/belonging-bullseye-strategy.

71. Thacker, Karissa. *The Art of Authenticity: Tools to Become an Authentic Leader and Your Best Self*. San Francisco: Berrett-Koehler Publishers, 2018.

72. Tractor Supply Company. *Tractor Supply Company Statement*. News release, 2024. https://corporate.tractorsupply.com/newsroom/news-releases/news-releases-details/2024/Tractor-Supply-Company-Statement/default.aspx.

73. US Census Bureau. *2017 National Population Projections Summary Tables*. Accessed February 21, 2025. https://www.census.gov/data/tables/2017/demo/popproj/2017-summary-tables.html.

74. World Intellectual Property Organization (WIPO). *Global Innovation Index 2024*. 2024. Accessed February 21, 2025. https://www.wipo.int/web-publications/global-innovation-index-2024/en/.

75. Workman, Valerie. "Bringing My Whole Self to Work at Tesla." *LinkedIn*, May 2020. https://www.linkedin.com/pulse/bringing-my-whole-self-work-tesla-valerie-workman-esq-/.

76. World Uncertainty Index. Accessed February 21, 2025. https://worlduncertaintyindex.com/.

77. Yoshino, Kenji. *Covering: The Hidden Assault on Our Civil Rights*. New York: Random House, 2006.

Acknowledgments

To everyone who helped us choose courage over fear.

Your belief in us and this message helped us step into the light when it would have been easy to succumb to the darkness of this moment—one that will certainly matter in our nation's history. Thank you.

To our families—especially our spouses, Chloe and Hillary. Thank you for your continued sacrifice. We know none of this has been easy or necessarily what you signed up for all those years ago. We couldn't have done this without you believing in us, working long hours to support us, and holding down the fort with the boys so we could join the Resistance.

To Ally Berthiaume—our incredible writing coach. Without you, this book would have been a pile of hot garbage. Thank you for the confidence, the structure, the discipline, the laughs, and the f-bombs. Choosing you was the best decision we made in this process. We're glad APG saved the best for last.

To our beta readers—Dan Pratte, Dr. Jacob Redding, Stefanie Santangelo, and Tori Tanaka. This version is a lot different, eh? That's only because you took the time to read our very rough beta version and gave us thoughtful feedback on how to make this book excellent and have the impact we all believed it could.

To Vanessa Shaw—our executive coach and our friend. Thank you for jumping on the Tesla train with us. We've come a long way from the initial goal of survival to now helping others have the courage to not live in survival mode. Our wild adventure together will help thousands of people. Thank you for helping us lean into our edge work, asking the difficult questions, and walking with us on our continued quest toward B'.

To our early advisers—Molly Caddam, Julie Cottingham, Rachel Kaplan, Liza Lipson, Robin Worthing Moon, Rosalie Nathans, Alexis Romero, and Bridget Seymour. We went through hell with many of you—whether at Tesla or in other formative moments in our lives—and we would do it again in a heartbeat. You believed in us when The Agency Initiative was only an outline of a speech. Thank you for your honest and candid counsel—for challenging us when we missed the mark and cheering us on every step of the way.

To Dr. Vijay Pendakur—an instant friend and mentor. Thank you for your generosity and willingness to share your experience in the publishing process with us. It gave us the confidence to step into this process when we needed it most.

Finally, and most importantly, thank you to our publishers— Amplify Publishing Group. You took a chance on us. We will never forget that.

About the Authors

Kristen Kavanaugh is the cofounder and CEO of The Agency Initiative, an Austin, Texas–based organizational effectiveness and leadership development consulting firm dedicated to creating a world with more leaders and organizations choosing courage in their most critical moments. She served as the vice chair of the Department of Defense's inaugural Defense Advisory Committee on Diversity and Inclusion until it was disbanded by the Trump administration in 2025. Previously, she served as the senior director of inclusion, talent, and learning at Tesla, where she led the diversity, equity, and inclusion, talent management, and learning and development functions for the global organization, formulating many of the ideas around courage and leadership during her nearly six-year tenure. Kristen holds a master's degree in social work from the University of Southern California in Los Angeles, California, and a bachelor's degree from the United States Naval Academy in Annapolis, Maryland.

Michael Randolph is the cofounder and COO of The Agency Initiative, where he helps leaders step into their agency and build values-driven organizations. Before launching The Agency Initiative,

Mike led talent experience at YETI and shaped leadership development and talent management at Tesla, integrating courageous leadership practices into the fabric of organizational growth. With over a decade of experience coaching senior leaders, he specializes in building resilient, people-centered cultures that thrive in uncertainty. Mike holds a master's degree in education from Purdue University and a bachelor's degree in international business and Asian studies from Augustana College. He has served on multiple professional development boards of directors for HR, talent development, and higher education. He believes leadership isn't about having all the answers—it's about having the courage to navigate the Moments That Matter.